# CALL

# OF THE

# SEA

Deb Haan    Sept 1. 2013

# CALL

# OF THE

# SEA

## Peter Haase

Fiction Publishing, Inc
Ft. Pierce, Florida

Copyright©2005 by Peter Haase
Second Edition


Fiction Publishing, Inc.
5626 Travelers Way
Ft. Pierce, Florida 34982
www.fictionpublishinginc.com

Printed in the United States of America

ISBN 978-09814956-9-9

# Call of the Sea
## Table of Contents

# Acknowledgments

I wish to extend my gratitude for the immeasurable help I received from the Morningside Writers Group, Port St. Lucie, Florida.

Special thanks are due to my daughter, Susanne, and to my son, Carlos, for their many helpful suggestions. Last, but certainly not least, I thank my daughter-in-law Linda, who provided the photo for the cover.

*He who goes to the sea*
*Leaves behind him all that is solid.*
*He leaves behind family and friends,*
*Familiar custom and language.*
*The rhythm of the seasons*
*No longer give him support.*
*Ahead of him lie the unknown*
*And the adventure,*
*And ahead lie solitude and isolation.*
*A human being,*
*Alone with himself,*
*Underway to ever new*
*And strange places.*

# Introduction

Nothing could keep us away from the sea. We were driven by our sense of adventure, propelled by the lure of the ocean and the freedom of which this vast, alien element spoke to us. Anything that floats—a raft, a plank, a tub, a barrel— would have served out purpose. A pair of oars or a paddle were symbols of escape. An upright pole from which to hang a piece of cloth to catch a breeze was a highly prized object in our juvenile imaginations, our desire for "leaving".

As often as possible, whenever we had a couple of marks, my friend Jürgen and I went down to the river and we rented a rowboat. *Vineta* was the boats name. We called her "die dicke Vineta" because of her bulky form.

Our river, the Warnow, was very wide—or so it seemed to us—and gave us plenty of interesting sites to explore. On the town side were the commercial piers where freighters of up to ten thousand tons loaded and unloaded cargo. The port of Rostock handled primarily grain and other agricultural products. There was a separate wharf at the coal depot. Lighters moved between anchored ships and the docks, carrying cargoes of building materials, lumber and machinery. It was not a large port, but a busy one. Fishing boats had their own little inner harbor, apart from the main port.

The ample, mile-long waterfront provided space for civic activities. In the summer, there were festivities with amusement park rides, food booths, beer and dance halls. Spring saw folklore displays and shows on improvised stages. In autumn, the farmers came to celebrate their harvest, the German version of Thanksgiving.

From 1933 onward, the festivities took on the more dubious forms of political propaganda affairs. Carefree merriment melted into somber events. Fierce speakers, with their arms stretched out in the Nazi salute, shouted slogans from the platforms. Flags and banners with the Swastika dominated the stages. Brown-shirted columns paraded along the wharf to the beat of marching bands. Later, field-gray replaced the brown shirts.

When World War II started in the fall of 1939, there were no more political rallies. Our daily lives changed little during the first years of successful campaigns. We could still rent "die dicke Vineta", just as in peacetime. Sometimes we rowed all the way to Gehlsdorf on the opposite bank of the Warnow. There was the Yacht Club. My brother, Dieter, three years my senior, had become a member and he sailed with his friends. At thirteen, Jürgen and I had to wait another year before we could join.

Air raids on German cities had been sporadic and no bombs fell on Rostock until 1942. Situated on the Warnow, this ancient port city of Hanseatic fame became a target in April of that year. In four consecutive nights, British bombers devastated our beloved town.

We lost our homes to the fires that swept through the city. Jürgen and his family had lived across the street from us. Eventually, we found new homes; Jürgen's family outside the city, we just around the corner from where we lived before. We had survived harrowing dangers and loved our wounded city with her rich maritime tradition even more.

Through the years, the Warnow remained our playground and sailing was our passion. Dieter sailed with his friends, Jürgen and I with like-minded boys and girls of our age group. Again and again we pointed the bows of our little sailboats between the jetties into the open sea, and every time the "Küstenwache", our Coast Guard, called us back. The military security zone, forbidden territory for non-essential craft, extended several miles from the harbor entrance into international waters. The war restricted our quest for the open ocean, for freedom and adventure.

One warm spring afternoon in 1945, I sailed for the last time on the Warnow.

Reluctantly, only days before the Soviet army took our town, we left our home and our friends behind, as did so many other families. Jürgen and I became separated until we found that both our families had escaped the *Russian Zone*. In the West, we enjoyed the freedom from political restrictions. Those who stayed behind merely exchanged the yoke of the Nazis for that of the Communists and found that there was little difference. Food and all other necessities were scarce for years on both sides of the invisible but all too present *Iron Curtain*.

In 1950, out of Kiel, Jürgen and I sailed with a small group of young men around the Danish islands in a chartered yacht. The Eastern part of the Baltic Sea was under the control of the Soviet Bloc. East European countries restricted access to their territorial waters for Western pleasure craft.

Rostock was beyond our reach for the next forty years.

# PRI HA GOFEN

My daughter, Susanne, had spoken to me of a certain Mister Ken Helprin, professor of psychology. She knew him from her days at New York University. One evening she said to me, "Dad, Ken Helprin is about to sail around the world. That's what you want to do with your retirement, right? Why don't you give him a call?"

Susanne often came up with great ideas. Two years before we had spent ten fantastic days in Tahiti, where we met a couple, passing through on a world cruise in their yacht *MON AMOUR*. Already then she had told me, "Dad, some day you will do that, believe me."

"Yeah, right," I had answered. "Things like that don't happen to me."

Now I thought, what the heck, give Ken Helprin a call. I once met him briefly at an open house or something at NYU. I dialed the number my daughter had given me.

"I remember you," he said kindly. Then he told me, "A friend of a friend of mine mentioned to me a certain

1

Aaron Orbin who is planning to sail around the world. I'm going to meet him this weekend in Wilmington, Delaware."

"Well," I said, "can I kind of come along? I just applied for my retirement and I wanted to sail around the world since I was a kid."

"Good idea. There is also a woman interested in joining, but Aaron is looking for one more person."

Ken had a deep, warm voice. He spoke slowly, as I imagined a profound thinker might speak. He sounded genuinely pleased. I knew from my daughter that he could be only a few years older than me, but he talked like an uncle would to a nephew, or a benevolent father to an overly enthusiastic son. His low, calm voice had a soothing quality.

I liked him, and my daughter had described him to me as a kind, generous and tolerant man.

I arranged to drive with him to Wilmington the next weekend to meet this man, Aaron Orbin.

So far in November of 1984, the weather had been benign. We met on a bright, sunny Saturday morning in front of my building on East 76th Street in Manhattan. His emaciated face, wispy beard and sparse shaggy hair were about a foot and a half above my eye level. Ken Helprin, six feet four inches tall, managed to fold his Quixote-like, loosely hinged body into the front passenger seat of my Honda Accord. I had pushed the seat back as far as it would go. I looked around for Rosinante and Sancho Panza on his burro, but I had only a brief glimpse of his middle-aged, matronly girlfriend, sitting behind the wheel of her Ford Escort, before she drove away.

Ken leaned back in his seat, with his knees against the dashboard. By the time we came out of the Lincoln Tunnel on the Jersey side, he was asleep.

I did not wake him until we reached the Delaware Bridge. "Where do we go from here?" I asked.

He gave me instructions as he had received them from Aaron Orbin. After stopping twice at gas stations in Wilmington to ask for directions, we found the apartment building where the Orbins resided.

Aaron was a ruggedly handsome man in his early sixties. He had recently retired from a research position at Dupont. The chemical giant had paid him a nice chunk of money for one of his inventions and he bought a thirty-eight foot ketch, a two-masted, cutter-rigged boat, which he named *PRI HA GOFEN*.

"What does it mean, Pri Ha Gofen?" I asked him after the initial introductions and some polite conversation. We had taken our seats in comfortable armchairs. A huge, black standard poodle lay at Aaron's feet. The living room was spacious and not cluttered with unnecessary furniture.

"It's the last line in a Hebrew prayer, at the end of which everyone raises his glass of kosher Manischewitz in a toast," he said with a patronizing smile. *Should I have known what it means?*

I did not have the impression that he was a religious man. So, why had he named his boat *PRI HA GOFEN?* Maybe it was his wife, Sylvia.

Sylvia, on the arm of a much younger woman, came and joined us. She was severely handicapped—from polio, I learned later. Her attractive face and stylish short, black hair were in striking contrast to her contorted body, barely capable of standing without something or someone to lean on. She spoke and conducted herself in a refined, dignified manner—graceful even in her gross deformity. Her husband by comparison was crude, almost boorish. The poodle didn't seem to mind.

The younger woman, Marge, with an interest in joining the world cruise of the *PRI HA GOFEN*, contributed little to the first talks concerning the voyage in planning. She was a sailor, though; had gathered some experience on the Chesapeake Bay and the Intracoastal Waterway.

We discussed the cost and the contribution of each crew member, the supplies and the provisioning, and the degree of our experiences.

Kenneth Helprin told us without bragging, for that was not his nature, that he had once crossed the Atlantic with an old seafarer. As an experiment they sailed without any instruments, not even a watch or a radio. He had joined the old mariner in the Cape Verde Islands and they ended up at Barbuda. I found out later that Ken had been seasick the entire three weeks at sea.

I explained that I had sailed since early childhood, that I practically grew up on the Baltic Sea. "I sailed around Denmark as a young man," I said. "Now I have a Cape Dory Typhoon and sail on the Hudson, in New York's inner and outer bays and Long Island Sound."

Aaron accepted my credentials readily. He himself, I soon realized, had no experience, except from books. He had studied navigation, learned all there is about boats, their construction and their maintenance. He educated himself in engines, self-steering and sextant observations, from interpreting the weather, to electronics and cooking on board. He knew more than Ken, the young woman and I combined—but only in theory. Well, he had tried out the ketch a couple of times on the Delaware. He was a scientist, and he approached the business of sailing around the world like a scientist: thoroughly, conscientiously and wisely.

We had tea, bread and cold cuts for supper and then talked until late at night. Sylvia took an active part in our planning. She contributed sound suggestions with regard to the itinerary. There were other participants, not present that evening, who would join in segments of the voyage. She mentioned a cousin, a stranger from Toronto and someone from Washington. Sylvia had an acute mind when and where one crew member would leave the boat, to be replaced by another.

I remember something like this: "Ken and Marge will be with you from the start. The three of you can manage until George gets there. He has two weeks in March and can fly to St. Thomas to meet you. When you get to Antigua, Frank will fly in from Toronto and replace him. Peter (that's me) will be available from early April and he will meet the boat in Guadeloupe. We are not sure yet if cousin Ben can make it, but I will spend some time on the boat with you at Fort de France in Martinique."

This woman had it all in her head, while mine was spinning out of control. I listened to her, not so much for what she was saying, but for her beautiful, refined diction. Her thought process was clear, her speech elegant, her tone melodious.

*She is going to fly to Martinique? How will she get there, and how will she get on the boat? Has she done this before? I mean, she can hardly walk unassisted. A remarkable woman.*

Aaron offered a nightcap. He served himself a tumbler of cognac, Ken had a whisky on the rocks and I drank scotch and soda. The women had already disappeared for the night.

Ken and I spent the night in a spare room. Aaron set up a cot and a mattress for us. Neither was long enough for Ken, so it did not matter which he chose. I ended up on the floor on the mattress. It had been a long day and we slept well, but in the morning Ken's feet were numb; they had been hanging over the end of the cot and the blanket was too short to cover them.

After a hearty breakfast, Aaron, Marge, Ken and I drove to the dock where we saw the *PRI HA GOFEN* for the first time. She did not strike me as particularly pretty. Her lines were rather clumsy instead of elegant. The high freeboard and large cabin trunk promised a roomy interior below decks. The hull was white, with blue boot top and trim. The bowsprit added four feet to her length of thirty-eight. This was a sturdy boat for blue-water cruising, not a beauty to show off at fancy yacht club regattas.

We stepped on board. The cockpit was short and functional. Nice woodwork and upholstery made the main cabin inviting. On the starboard side of the companionway, there was the galley with a four-burner propane stove and oven. The captain's quarters, a bedroom with a sliding door, was on port. The ample beam of the vessel allowed for a couch with an athwartship extension along the bulkhead, and a settee on the opposite side. A fixed dining table sat in the middle. Forward of the main cabin, or the saloon, was the head with built-in shower, washbasin and all the amenities of home, albeit somewhat reduced in size. The forepeak, also called the fo'c'sle, is usually sleeping quarters for the crew.

We nodded our approval. This was a boat to take us around the world, all right. Not too fancy, not too austere. Aaron gave us a rundown of the equipment, the storage areas, safety devices and the engine department. "This is an eighty horsepower Westerbeke Diesel. A big engine. You could call this boat a motor-sailer, if she had an indoor wheel house."

I didn't like that. I want a sailboat to be a sailboat.

We sat in the saloon and talked about the duties on board, who's in charge of this and of that. It all seemed a bit too formal to me. Too many rules, too strict divisions of duties and resposabilities reduce the fun and tend to produce friction, quarrels and unhappiness. It occurred to me that Aaron could become a difficult man to deal with. I thought at the time that Ken and Marge also felt a little intimidated by Aaron's overbearing personality.

We returned to the apartment for lunch. Sylvia had ordered a paella from a Spanish restaurant. She set the table with fine china and exquisite silverware. The meal as excellent and Marge kept filling the crystal goblets with cool sangria from an antique pewter pitcher.

I returned to New York alone. Ken and Marge were the crew for the first leg of the voyage and they had more to discuss about their roles in this enterprise. It was the middle of November, and the voyage was to start at the beginning of the new year.

I was euphoric over the prospect of an extended ocean cruise; I drove ninety miles an hour on the New Jersey Turnpike on my way back to New York.

The first item on my list of business was to put my my Cape Dory up for sale. The boat was already out of the water for the winter. She sat in her cradle in the yard of the Barren Island Marina in Brooklyn. Washed down and in generally in good shape, I expected to get a fair price. But who would want to buy a boat in the dead of winter?

I placed an ad in the New York Times classified section for the last weekend in November and received no calls. I let it run again the first Saturday in December. I got one call.

"What do you want for the boat?" A Brooklyn macho voice came through the line.

"Three thousand. She's in excellent condition."

"What? you must be crazy! Three thousand? The boat is almost ten years old."

"Come and take a look at her. I'm sure we can make a deal."

*The only call. I've got to sell the boat.*

We arranged to meet an evening during the week. I put a ladder against the hull and turned down the plastic cover to allow access to the cockpit and the cabin.

"Take a good look at her. She's in fine shape, inside and out," I told the man.

He looked at the keel and then walked to the other side. "Two thousand cash," he said and didn't even bother to climb the ladder.

*I can't lose him.* "All right, but that's without the motor." I made one last attempt at saving face.

"With the motor. Take it or leave it. I'm not in the mood to hassle."

"You drive a hard bargain. Got yourself a deal. You have the money on you?"

He pulled a wad of twenties from his pocket and handed it to me. In the almost dark, cold evening, out there in the boat yard, I counted fifty bills.

"That's only a thousand," I said. *Is he trying to pull a fast one on me?*

From his other pocket he extracted ten crisp one hundred dollar bills. "Here's the rest. I need the registration and a bill of sale."

We went back to my car and I took the registration from my wallet. On a piece of paper he scribbled *...sold to...Cape Dory, as is, where is, US$500...*

"Here, sign this. I don't want to pay sales tax on the full amount."

"Okay," I said. I didn't care. I did the same when I bought the boat nearly seven years before.

Without another word, he went back to his car and took off. I felt pretty good. Sure, he took advantage of me, but what choice did I have? I never received another response to my ad. Who buys a boat in the middle of winter in New York?

I specified my retirement date to be the last day in February 1985. After the sale of my boat, I had ten weeks to coordinate my responsibilities at the office. I had been in charge of seafood import and distribution for a large Far Eastern company and concentrated on the transfer of my work to my successor.

My announcement to give up my apartment as of 15 March came as a surprise to my landlord. He was pleased, though, that I gave him three months notice. I had lived there for more than six years, the last two and a half by myself.

On the last Friday of February, my coworkers staged a farewell party. The company had never seen anything like it. There were hors d'oeuvres and salads, shrimp, lobster and caviar, beer, champagne and everything in between, including my favorite scotch, Black Label. Nearly all of the more than four hundred staff crowded into the conference room next to my office. Both my children, Susanne and Carlos, were present as special guests.

In my brief speech I said, "Although I am giving up my job after almost twenty-four years with the company, I am not retiring. I am just changing my lifestyle."

My landlord allowed me to leave my furniture, if I had no place to store them. *The Cat*, my girlfriend of many years, who had originally shared the apartment with me, now lived in Brooklyn. She had little room—and little interest—in things we had once bought together. We remained good friends, in spite of a stormy break-up. I stayed at her place for the next two weeks.

The only possessions I could take on my adventure fitted into a duffel bag and a small knapsack.

"The Cat, can't you keep my suits, shirts and shoes in your storage room?" I asked her and added with a crooked smile, "It's only gonna be for three years." She had earned her nickname *The Cat* for her feline nature.

"Yeah, all right. I guess I owe you that much," she answered playfully, as if making a huge sacrifice.

"It's only two boxes. Hardly anything. No big deal, you see?" I gave her a big hug. "Thanks."

While The Cat went to her job as a receptionist in midtown, I ran last-minute errands. Business friends and my Japanese coworkers had given me a total of four watches as parting gifts, in addition to the one I already had. I set out to the Jewelry Exchange at the Bowery and Canal Street, and sold three of them. I kept only the Seiko *Silver Wave*, sent to me from Tokyo, and the Pulsar dress watch, a Christmas gift from my children.

I stayed in close contact with Sylvia Orbin. The *PRI HA GOFEN* departed on a cold day in mid-January, reached the warm waters of the Gulf Stream in a few days and arrived in San Juan, Puerto Rico, on 3 February.

There was trouble almost from the start. I received reports that Ken was seasick from the time they left the Chesapeake Bay. Marge panicked when they hit rough weather east of Turks and Caicos. Arguments ensued and Ken left the *PRI HA GOFEN* the moment they reached San Juan. Aaron and Marge sailed alone to St. Thomas.

That put me in a dilemma. Would I have to join Aaron without Ken? I had already quit my job and given notice to my landlord. I couldn't stay with The Cat in her small studio apartment. My last instructions were to buy a plane ticket to Pointe-a-Pitre, Guadeloupe, and I had already booked a flight from JFK for 28 March. I no longer had a choice in the matter.

Sylvia asked me to take out an ad in the New York Times for "someone interested in a month-long cruise in the Caribbean on a private yacht." I received two inquiries. Both were from men in their thirties, both without experience, one was straight, the other obviously gay. The straight one could not fit the schedule into his time frame, which left me with the gay one.

Both Aaron and Sylvia gave their okay, and I sent him out to St. Thomas. Sylvia worked hard to coordinate the availability of the remaining potential crew, but in the end it turned out that no one could make it.

Aaron, Marge and the gay guy sailed from St. Thomas to Antigua—and that's as far as they got. Marge couldn't take it anymore and Aaron threw out the gay guy. There was no way that Aaron alone could sail the boat to Pointe-a-Pitre in time to meet me there on the 28th. Sylvia flew to Antigua to accompany her husband on that leg of the trip.

I am not sure I got the story right, but what does it matter? The whole thing fell apart. Not a good start for me, I thought. What have I gotten myself into?

When I arrived in the evening of 28 March in Pointe-a-Pitre, nobody was there to meet me. I sat in the small arrivals building with my two bags. All passengers and personnel had left.

The cleaning crew came in. They spoke French. I didn't. I thought of calling The Cat, just to talk so someone. *But, why bother her? It's my problem.*

After two hours I managed to leave a note with a security guard, addressed to Aaron. "Went to find hotel. Meet you here at nine in the morning. Peter."

At that time, Aaron stormed into the deserted terminal. "Oh good, you're still here. I circled Monserrat, thought it was Guadeloupe. Got here as fast as I could. Boat's on the other side. I have a taxi waiting. Let's go."

The *PRI HA GOFEN* lay at anchor in a shallow bay. The Taxi dropped us off at a small wooden dock where Aaron had left the dinghy. We stowed my bags in the bow, I got into the stern. Aaron manned the oars and rowed us out to the boat.

Sylvia was on board, propped up in the corner of the settee. "Peter! I am so happy to see you!" she called out as I came down the companionway into the cabin.

I was glad to see her too. I was not looking forward to life with Aaron alone.

They welcomed me with a glass of kosher wine and I wondered, would I be expected to eat kosher? I knew words like lahaime, Manishevits, masletov—not the spelling, though, obviously—and that was the extent of my knowledge of all things Jewish.

Aaron heated up a portion of leftover Bulgar. "Hungry?" he asked me, and I must have said yes.

He served me a thick mess of Bulgar, a food in my opinion not made for human consumption, concocted of some grain in middle-Eastern fashion. It was Aaron's specialty and he prepared it often. I never got used to it.

Soon after my arrival on the boat, I crept into my bunk in the fo'c'sle. It was after midnight and it had been quite a day for me. My good-bye from The Cat had been bittersweet, quick and tearless. My flight to Puerto Rico, as well as the three-hour wait in San Juan and my connecting flight to Pointe-a-Pitre were uneventful. By the time Aaron showed up, it was long dark.

I went to sleep with the soft gurgling and splashing sound wavelets make against the hull—my first night in Caribbean waters.

In the morning we raised the anchor. The *PRI HA GOFEN* had an electric winch. I was amazed at how Sylvia moved about the boat. She made the coffee, toasted and buttered bread, and fried eggs with bacon. What astounded me even more was how she managed to haul herself up the companionway into the cockpit.

On our way to the port of Pointe-a-Pitre she handled the wheel expertly while Aaron was consulting the chart. It seemed, the only thing she could not do was walk or stand without holding on to someone or something.

One more thing amazed me about her: how she kept her composure when Aaron treated her rudely and answered her with undeserved gruffness. Sometimes he seemed to despise her.

Without being meek or intimidated, she said no more than, "I wish you would not speak to me like that," or "you really have no reason to be so angry with me, Aaron." This seemed to have an effect on him; he promptly mended his attitude toward her and spoke in a calmer, friendlier way.

We remained five days in exotic, colorful Pointe-a-Pitre. We had anchored in the central harbor, a busy place with launches and barges speeding their way to and fro. The docks were piled disorderly with crates and baskets containing fruits and vegetables. Barefooted men with pushcarts moved among them, hollering in unfamiliar language.

In an adjacent marketplace, women in aprons and brightly colored turbans sold fish and produce that was unprotected from the heat and the sun. Flies buzzed about the stands, crates and tubs filled with goods.

Since going ashore involved the use of the dinghy, I was not quite independent. We determined when to meet at the dinghy landing place for the ride back to the boat. Once on land, I strolled around town by myself. At a bank I exchanged dollars for the Caribbean franks, the currency of the French islands in the Lesser Antilles. I ate Creole meals in rustic places—better than Bulgar—and bought a case of Red Stripe beer, brewed in Jamaica. It never became one of my favorites.

On our last day in Pointe-a-Pitre, Aaron, carrying his wife in his arms, slipped on the wet concrete steps that led down to the dinghy. Both fell into the water polluted with garbage. I was already in the dinghy, holding it steady, and stretched out a hand in an attempt to help. Aaron, recovering, pushed me roughly aside, got a foothold on the steps and dragged Sylvia out of the water. At last, drenched, they made it into the dinghy.

I didn't know what to say or how to act. Knowing Aaron's disagreeable disposition, I said nothing and acted as if nothing had happened. That was probably the best course of action, or inaction. They were both unharmed and none of us ever mentioned this unpleasant incident.

The following morning, Aaron hired a taxi and took his wife to the airport for her flight back home.

Now I was alone with Aaron, a situation I did not care for. He always appeared to me in conflict with himself. Any conversation seemed to be an effort for him; he was often silent for hours and I did not interrupt the silences. Little did he succeed in covering up what I determined to be a deep-rooted frustration. At our first meeting back in November, I overheard the two women and learned that Sylvia had polio in her childhood. Aaron had married her as a cripple. He burdened himself with this woman and thereby crippled himself. Robust and athletic, he deprived himself of living a full life.

How did this healthy, vigorous man come to marry a severely handicapped woman? Desirable as she was in all other than physical aspects, he had to be a martyr. Did he think, as a young man, that he could handle it, only to find himself later incapable? Did he curse his youthful mistake? Was the guilt of being unable to carry the burden serenely overpowering him?

We left Guadeloupe and stopped for the night at the Isle des Saints, a short distance away. In the morning we rowed ashore and landed the dinghy on the narrow beach of this small, rocky island.

"You want to come along, do some climbing?" Aaron asked me.

Nice of him to ask, I thought. "Yes, a little exercise might be good."

We found a path that skirted the steep, central mountain peak, went over rough terrain and followed along the side of vertical precipices. Often there was no path at all

14

and we had to find our way, climbing sheer rock. Aaron walked at a fast pace. I had considerable difficulty keeping up with him. I was totally exhausted when after two and a half hours we arrived back at the dinghy landing place.

This must be how he deals with his pent-up frustration, I thought; his unused energy.

We sailed south to the next island, Dominica. Before we had come close enough to drop anchor off the beach near Portsmouth, a swarm of small boats came out to meet us.

Men and boys, wildly gesticulating and shouting, raced each other to get to us. They rowed and paddled, few had an outboard motor, some swam. A welcoming committee? Far from it. Fights broke out among them for the right to do business with us. Older men pushed boys aside; stronger kids bullied the little ones.

They came alongside. We had to use boathooks and oars to keep them from climbing aboard.

The situation was scary. I would have turned back out to sea, but Aaron did not let them intimidate him.

"Drop the anchor, Peter," he called out to me.

I put down the boathook with which I had armed myself and went forward to release the chain from the capstan. The anchor went down.

Aaron selected three or four young men from the belligerent crowd. "I will deal only with you," he told them, "but first you have to get rid of all the others."

Clever strategy, I thought, and little by little they succeeded sending most of the others back to shore.

Aaron took a stern line to the beach and tied it to a tree. A young boy continued to hang around.

"I cut your line, mon," he threatened. "You give me no job, no money, no nothin', I swear I cut your line."

Aaron was undeterred. He negotiated only with the four men who were proud of their special status. In the end

15

he struck a deal with them to buy some coconuts, mangoes and bananas.

They took Aaron and me to the shore in their large canoe with outrigger, which reminded me of Polynesia. We entered a narrow creek and they gave us a tour through a veritable rain forest. The winding waterway led to a couple of thatched huts. Women, some with babies in their arms, stood around and marveled at the strangers who had come to visit.

Loaded with a bagful of mangoes, two coconuts and several hands of still green bananas, they took us back to our boat. After a short hassle over the amount of money, they went back to shore. The aggressive kid was hanging out on the beach. I still felt nervous about the threats he had made.

"You owe me two bucks," Aaron said to me. I gladly paid him. I would rather eat bananas than bulgar.

I was relieved to find all our lines intact in the morning. We motored the short distance to Roseau, the capital of Dominica.

Since independence from Great Britain seven years before, this island nation sank deep into poverty. Dominica is among the poorest in the Caribbean.

We got our passports stamped in the Government office in Roseau. Aaron inquired for a tour of the rain forest and found a taxi driver willing to take him into the mountains. I was not interested in an expedition into the jungle.

"I have seen enough selvas when I lived in Ecuador," I told Aaron. "I prefer to stay in town, eat and drink something local, see what life is like here. I am not much of a nature guy." I wanted to spend some time away from him and not end up again climbing mountains for hours, as we did on Les Saints.

Roseau, I found, was not much of a town. I saw no great mansions or palaces of past splendor. If there were any cathedrals of significance, I missed them. I saw neither museums nor monuments. I found no pretty park or plaza, no statue with some hero on a rearing horse. Roseau was a ramshackle accumulation of houses. Some were built of concrete or stone, but most were of plastered or whitewashed bamboo.

*Dominicans, forgive me! I guess I missed all the greatness of which I am sure you have plenty to be proud of.*

Aaron must have enjoyed his excursion into the inner regions of the island. He returned more relaxed, less tense. The hard lines in his face had softened.

"I had a fascinating ride up the mountain. I encouraged the driver to take the side roads and had to give him an extra ten dollars to drive over gravel and pothole-strewn jungle paths. I saw a banana and a coffee plantation. We stopped in the middle of the rain forest and I walked, inhaled the fragrant, humid air and listened to the sounds of the creatures." He seemed a changed man. "The rickety old car made it all right. How was your day?"

"I am glad you enjoyed yourself. I must have walked every street of Roseau, even into the outskirts. Found nothing remarkable. A lot of poverty. The food is bad, but I liked the fried plantains. I found no local beer, had to drink that awful Red Stripe." My report sounded dismal compared to his, so I added, "The colorful market place was interesting."

That evening it was my turn to cook. I made a simple dish of spaghetti with clam sauce, followed by some white cheese and bread I had bought in Roseau.

After dinner, Aaron fell back into his brooding mood. He picked up a book, lay down on the couch and didn't say another word. The day in town and the tropical heat had tired me and I went to sleep right after I had finished with the dishes.

In the morning, Aaron gave me no clue what his plan was. He did not communicate his thoughts on a timetable or which islands to visit next. The entire day he did not speak a word, just lay on the couch, reading or dozing.

*Is he thinking of going ashore again to day? Will he want to use the dinghy? What should I do? What an awkward situation.*

I busied myself doing some laundry, picked up a book and wrote my impressions in a notebook.

The last time I heard from Ken Helprin was when he left the *PRI HA GOFEN* in San Juan. "I am going to the Virgin Islands to look around for a boat I could buy," he had told me and asked me to come down and join him instead of Aaron. "That man is such an ass, he will make your life miserable, I tell you." I now understood what he meant.

Sylvia gave me a different story. Ken had been so seasick that he made a mess of the boat and disgusted everybody on board. Marge had threatened to quit unless they got rid of Ken. Sylvia could not give me a reason why Marge later left Aaron in Antigua.

Still anchored at Roseau, I began to ponder what the near and extended future held for me. Three years alone with Aaron, sailing around the world? That seemed a harsh sentence to me. There had to be other options.

"Today we sail to Martinique," Aaron announced. He had finally come out of his lethargy.

All right, I thought, at last some action. He never consulted me or discussed his plans.

In Fort de France, we docked the boat in a marina adjacent to the commercial harbor. We were back in a more civilized part of the world. Most of the yachts in the marina were French and the whole atmosphere was French. The language we heard, the signs we read, the billboards— French, French, French.

18

The docking was the "stern-to" method, popular in the Mediterranean. With the boat's stern tied to the dock, an anchor keeps the bow perpendicularly away. Aaron maneuvered into position and backed toward the dock, while I handled the anchor chain, stopping the boat just a foot or two from the dock. The marina attendant provided a gangplank to get ashore.

That evening, Aaron had a kind word for me. "Peter, you did a pretty good job with that anchor today," he said.

I was speechless.

In this town I had considerable freedom to come and go as I pleased. I hung out with the crews from other boats, trying my shamefully deficient French. There was one large motor yacht from Amsterdam, with Dutch, German and Spanish crew.

Aaron heard me talking with them in German and Spanish. "I didn't know you were so talented in languages," he commented. I told him that I had lived in Ecuador and he knew, of course, that I was German.

Fort de France was cosmopolitan, larger and more European than Pointe-a-Pitre. Still, it had something of a colonial stamp on it, as a tropical island capital. But, walking the streets of this city, I did not have the feeling that I was in an exotic place.

Store and shop windows exhibited goods of fine qualities. I saw the same brand names as in France, Germany or the United States. Banks and multi-storied office and apartment buildings did not look different from any mid-sized town on the continent. During the lunch hour or after business hours, shoppers hurried as they do anywhere else.

In the multitude of local islanders I found an astonishing number of well-dressed men and elegantly attired ladies.

The open market was not as chaotic as those in some places we had visited, but equally as colorful. Scenes Gauguin had painted over a century ago came to mind. The bright colors, the women in aprons and headscarves, selling fruit and vegetables to ladies with huge feathers on their hats.

At a souvenir stand I found reproductions of Gauguin's painting on placemats. I bought a set of four of them for Susi. Back at the marina a peddler showed me some bracelets, made of coral. I selected a highly polished brown one, with beautiful golden-yellow streaks. The Cat might like this one, I thought.

I stepped over the plank onto the transom. Aaron sat in the cabin, bent over a book, just as I had left him earlier that day. Has he been in town, I wondered?

"Very nice town, Fort de France," I ventured.

"Hmm." He gave no indication that he had even been off the boat.

"I ate in a nice restaurant. Lamb chops, yellow rice, a salad and French bread."

He did not respond and kept reading.

I picked up a can of beer from the refrigerator, took one of the cigars I had bought and sat on a bench at the dock. Some people stopped for chitchat. If someone had asked me where we were going next, I would have had to answer, "I don't know. The boss doesn't talk."

Fort de France had been one of the scheduled stops. I was looking forward to visit St. George's on the island of Grenada. It was entirely up to Captain Aaron Orbin when we would get there, and he didn't talk.

On the morning of the third day in Fort de France, it suddenly occurred to him. "Let's get out of here. Long enough in this place," without the least concern that I might want to stay another day, or that I had some idea of my own.

20

I gave myself the time to finish my cereal and coffee and then went forward to tend to the anchor. Within minutes of announcing that we were leaving, we were underway.

Southbound, in the chain of islands, St. Lucia, St. Vincent and the Grenadines were next in line. Grenada was last before Trinidad and Tobago.

Just a couple of hours out of the marina, Aaron decided to stop at St. Anne. We anchored in the cul-de-sac in front of Club Med, but we did not go ashore. The dinghy remained tied down on the foredeck. There was all the fun a short ride away, but we sat on the damn boat, not talking to each other. *This man is impossible.*

I went forward to sit on the upturned dinghy, listened to the music that came over from Club Med, and smoked a cigar. *To hell with Aaron.*

We motored out of the cul-de-sac in the morning and promptly got stuck on a sandbank.

"Give her power, Peter. Full throttle!" How did he know we would reach deeper water? Well, he did. With the keel cutting a furrow in the sandy bottom, the boat crossed the shallow spot and we were on our way to St. Lucia.

I had read about St. Lucia and St. Vincent in the Cruising Guide and elsewhere. Both islands were well worth a visit, but evidently Aaron did not think so. Without a word or an explanation, we passed them by—both of them. *What is the matter with this man?*

We sailed a day and a night, and another half day, admittedly in a beautiful east wind of eighteen knots, and anchored off the tiny islet of Carriacou. Besides having a spectacular view—rocks rising straight out of the ocean, reaching a height of over a hundred feet—there was nothing to do at this place. For how long can you look at rocks, no matter how breathtaking they may be? Waves crashing into them, birds circling, the sun setting over them? We stayed for a day and a half, not talking to each other.

The boat rocked in the heavy surf. All night I was tossed about in the V-berth, not knowing what was going on in *Captain Ahab's* mind.

At last we made the short hop into St. George's, capital of Grenada, the harbor, squared off at three sides with concrete embankments, open to the west.

Local boats and small freighters occupied the berths along the seawalls. Harbor Control advised us to tie up on one of the moorings in the middle of the harbor.

Grenada is one of the smaller islands in the chain of the Lesser Antilles, and the one farthest south. We had reached the end of the first leg of our world cruise.

The question of crew seemed all but forgotten since Sylvia flew home from Guadeloupe. I had an ambiguous feeling about the future of our voyage. There were several possibilities, but I could not read Aaron's mind.

We could sail to the Virgin Islands or Puerto Rico and from there across the Atlantic via Bermuda and the Azores. Or, we could go all the way north along the US coast, taking advantage of the Gulf Stream. The rhumb line would take us to Ireland, the English Channel or Northern France. Another option would be to sail south, via Trinidad and Tobago, avoiding the approaching hurricane season, and head down the East coast of South America. Then we could cross the South Atlantic to Cape Town.

But what about crew? Just Aaron and me? I did not like that prospect at all. I am a mellow fellow, but I have my threshold. At some point the bizarre behavior of that man would no longer be tolerable. For the time being, I was at his mercy.

My last chance to leave the *PRI HA GOFEN* had been in Fort de France. I could have found a place on another yacht, but at that time such a thought had not yet occurred to me.

St. George's clings to a steep hill that overlooks the harbor. From the boat we had a splendid view of the town. Aaron showed no interest in going ashore, but we had to take the dinghy in to report to the authorities. He returned right away to the boat.

"I will find my way back later. I'll pay someone to take me back," I said to him, implying that I'd rather spend my time in town than with him on the boat. If he got the message, he didn't show it.

The streets were neat, washed down by frequent downpours. The market place near the harbor was vibrant and colorful, the language English, or I should say British.

Grenada, the spice and perfume island, offered excellent shopping. I ate fish and chips at the market and had a glass of ale. I climbed the steep streets and dodged a sudden shower with other passersby beneath a storefront.

European and beautiful Creole women crowded the busy streets and shops. Gentlemen in business attire sat at lunch counters. Tradesmen with pushcarts called out their merchandise for sale.

A motor launch was preparing to leave from the dinghy landing place. "Sorry to be a nuisance, but would it be too much trouble to drop me off at the boat you see in the middle of the harbor?" I tried to sound British. "There's a good chap."

"Hop in, hop in! No bother at all. Glad to do it. Always pleased to give a hand. One hand washes the other, that's what I say. If one gentleman can't help another, where does that leave us? No no, keep those bills in your pocket. You might need them. Here we are already. Careful now, as you step aboard. Cheerio, my good man!"

"Much obliged." I still tried to sound British. *What a wonderful specimen of a Grenadian.*

Aaron was even gloomier, more introspective that evening. He did not inquire how my day was. Dirty dishes in the sink indicated that he had eaten supper. He was reading and hardly looked up as I entered.

My "hi" remained unanswered. *Boy, he is getting so bad. Where will this end?*

I sat in the cockpit for a while, then went into my bunk in the forepeak, read a few pages and soon fell asleep.

In the morning he said calmly, perhaps with forced calm, "Let's get out of here. Peter, you untie us from the buoy. We tow the dinghy."

With the dinghy in tow, I knew we weren't going far. Barely out of the harbor, he turned south and half an hour later we dropped the anchor just off the beach.

American forces, for whatever reason, had invaded the island in 1983. Outside the town, there were still signs of limited warfare: a burnt-out tank, a bunker riddled with shrapnel marks, an abandoned machine gun position.

The sight seemed to animate him. "You see that? This is where the battle took place. We were right to go in."

I didn't want to get into politics with him. I had not followed that conflict and had no idea whether it was right or wrong. Besides, I had no clue of Aaron's political views and no interest to find out, so I remained quiet.

I opened a can of corned beef, put bread on the table and sat down to eat. Aaron joined me. When I got up to get a can of beer from the refrigerator, he asked me, "Get me one too, will you?"

I had never seen him drinking beer before.

By three o'clock he said, "Help me get the dinghy on board. We'll sail for the Dominican Republic. It's a long haul."

24

"Okay," I answered and brought the dinghy forward so that we could attach the halyard to it and hoist it onto the foredeck. As soon as it was in place and tied down, Aaron worked the winch and the anchor came up. *Good to be underway.*

A fine easterly breeze was blowing and we rolled out the mainsail and the Genoa. He told me the course to steer, then went below to punch the coordinates into the SatNav, the Satellite Navigation System.

This was more like it. He even spoke to me and I knew where we were going. I was happy to be sailing, and in the right direction.

What his plans were, once we got there—I didn't care. I would get off this boat. He would have to look for another crew.

I connected the helm to the windvane, the mechanical steering device, and sat back.

Years after our divorce, Julia and I decided that we weren't really such bad people. We had split up and blamed each other; however, in the long run, we could not ignore the fact that we both had good qualities.

I knew that Julia's trustworthiness was beyond reproach, and during my absence she handled my money matters. That was not as big a deal as it might seem. My pension went directly into my account, from which Julia paid my credit card bills and reimbursed herself for the collect calls I ran up on her phone card number. That was pretty much it.

I had telephoned her from Grenada and informed her of my dilemma. She had foreseen trouble from the start, as soon as Kenneth Helprin quit.

"You and this Aaron guy alone on the boat now?" she asked. "That's a problem, I tell you. You plan to sail across the ocean alone with him?" She couldn't even know how big a problem that would be.

"I don't think so," I had answered. "He never tells me about his plans, but just the two of us—that would be suicide."

"He might be crazy enough to start out before you know it. Be careful."

Then I had called The Cat. "I am in Grenada. I don't know when we are leaving and where we're going next."

She said, "Oh well, let me know when you get there."

"Get where? I have no idea where we're going."

"Europe. Isn't that where you're going? You told me. See, I listen."

"I don't think you heard a word I was saying. The man is a lunatic!"

"Yeah, I know. You told me. I gotta go. Have an appointment at the hair salon. Mmmmbah!" She sent me a kiss through the line and hung up.

*I am fond of one, but in love with the other.* Be that as it may, I was stuck with Aaron in his *PRI HA GOFEN* somewhere in the Caribbean, four days away from the Dominican Republic.

Night fell. The wind freshened and the seas built to six to eight feet. Aaron was below, reading, napping. He hardly ever showed up on deck. So far we have had no need to agree on watches, alternating every three or four hours at the helm. Now it was a different story; we had to cover five hundred nautical miles of ocean. Did he expect me to be on watch four or five days non-stop?

At midnight I went below and told him, "I am going to bed."

He said, "Okay." That was it. He didn't seem to care.

The boat behaved well, the windvane was doing a good job, but shouldn't someone be out there? Could he be so irresponsible? Did he not care at all?

Sleep in the V-berth is nearly impossible when the vessel is underway. The bow smashes into waves, is knocked about, rises and falls. A body in the forepeak is now airborne, now pressed down hard on the mattress.

I got up, made a cup of coffee, and then sat again behind the wheel on the helmsman's chair. Several times I went below, to the head, to look at the SatNav or to get a snack. Aaron did not go to bed. He did not move from the corner of the couch where he sat, reading.

For the next two days, I had only now and then a few moments of fitful sleep. On the third day, the wind backed to the north and increased to forty knots. I advised Aaron to reef the mainsail and roll up some of the Genoa. Without questioning, he came on deck and winched one third of the big sail into the mast. The boat had this great, sophisticated space-age furling system. I rolled up a portion of the headsail. This reduced our speed noticeably and we were sailing a comfortable close reach.

Aaron went below again. Twenty minutes later, he came halfway up the companionway.

"I meant to talk to you, Peter. I did a lot of thinking these last few days. We are going back to the States, via Puerto Rico. New course 345 degrees."

That hit me like the proverbial ton of bricks. My answer was stuck in my throat. He did not wait for an answer and went back down into the cabin.

I had to digest what just happened. I wanted to get off the boat anyway. What better place than Puerto Rico? Back to the States was no option for me. "Three years around the world," I had told everyone. How could I show my face in New York after just one month? I had to find another boat.

I enjoyed sailing this heavy boat in the strong conditions. *If only I weren't so damn tired. No sleep for days. I am like an automaton. My nerves are twitching. My mind shuts off for seconds at a time. Tomorrow evening we will be in San Juan. Maybe I can sleep then. Wait a minute: Ken Helprin. I must get in touch with Ken Helprin!*

Now that he told me his decision, Aaron seemed to have unburdened himself of something that had oppressed him. Maybe he felt he owed me more of an explanation. He returned to the companionway.

"I thought this was what I wanted to do." He said. "Sailing, see the world. But it's not. These backward places, the poverty, the primitive circumstances in these islands—I've had enough of that."

This seemed odd to me. He had read so much, seen pictures; the Cruising Guide books are full of what the islands are like. Why did that come as a surprise to him? Most people go cruising to get away from *our* world.

I didn't know how best to respond and just shrugged my shoulders. I had made up my mind and didn't care about him anymore. *From now on, I look after myself.*

He went on, "Besides, I miss my dog." After a while, "And my wife and my home." *In that order?*

Now I knew the real reason. I had figured him out. He lived in a world he didn't like. He carried the burden of his crippled wife on his mind wherever he went, what ever he did, then felt guilty that he felt that way. He tried to escape and couldn't do it. Disappointment, frustration, guilt. I should have felt sympathy for him, but I did not.

Then came another punch line. "I am going to put the boat up for sale."

The last night before reaching San Juan, we had to do some island dodging. The lights of Vieques were in sight by eleven o'clock and Aaron joined me in the cockpit. He had done all the navigation so far.

I was fed up with blindly following his instructions, so I insisted on looking at the chart myself. Along the east coast of Puerto Rico, at Roosevelt Roads and around the island of Vieques, there were areas for US Navy maneuvers and target bombing. These zones are marked on the nautical charts as "restricted".

Between midnight and three a m we sailed through the Vieques Passage and, with the first light of the new day, we passed Isla Palominos. After rounding Cape San Juan, we had clear sailing.

In the early afternoon we entered the port of San Juan.

El Morro, the monumental, ancient fortress stands on the eastern approach into the harbor. On the same side, a mile or so past the customs office, we found docking space at the concrete embankment.

It was Sunday. People strolled by, watching cruise ships and cargo vessels entering and leaving port. In the adjacent park, families lolled on the ample lawns; children ran along the curving paths. Occasionally, rambling pedestrians stopped to look at and comment on the yacht that had arrived.

Aaron and I walked over to the Customs office to clear in. He had to fill out a few forms, and we were again in US territory. Back on board, I tried to catch up on my sleep, but a question occupied my mind: what now?

The fo'c'sle was stifling hot in the still air of the afternoon. For a while I sat in the cockpit. Pedestrians, who wanted to know this and that about the boat, interrupted my thought process. They asked where we had been, where we were going, how many there were on board and so on. I made an effort to give polite answers and to satisfy their curiosity, but I was so damn tired. *Where do I go from here?*

*Kenneth Helprin. Did he buy a boat in the Virgin Islands? Where could I find him?* In my address book I had the name and number of a Mister Golden, lawyer friend of Ken. Maybe he knew Ken's whereabouts. It was a long shot, but I should try it before venturing out to St. Thomas to find one person who might or might not have bought a boat recently.

I walked to the nearby ferry dock where I found a phone booth and called The Cat. There was no answer.

When I came back to the boat, Aaron was busy with the water hose. "Peter, help me with this. There is a faucet outside the public bathrooms over there. Hook up the hose so we can fill the tanks. The hose is just long enough."

This would be the last job I do on his *PRI HA GOFEN*. "Okay," I said, picked up the end of the hose and walked with it to the bathhouse. I connected the hose to the faucet and on his signal turned the water on.

Then I returned to the boat. "Aaron, I am not sailing back to the States with you. I'll get off the boat tomorrow morning. I joined you to sail, in a pleasant atmosphere, with one or two more crew on a long voyage. None of that happened."

I went back to the faucet, waited for him to let me know when to turn off the water.

Later, as he rolled up the hose, he said to me, "My decision has nothing to do with you. You are a good shipmate."

"I know your decision has nothing to do with me. You make your decisions without concern for anyone else. By the way, you owe me forty dollars I paid ahead for the eight days left in this month."

I returned to the phone booth on the ferry dock. The Cat answered my call.

"Peter? Where are you? In San Juan? How's the weather?

"Never mind the weather. Look, there is something I want you to do. Will you please call Mister Golden at this number? Got a pencil?"

"Wait. Okay, go ahead. What do you want me to tell him, and who is he?"

"He is a friend of Ken Helprin's. Ask him where I can find Ken, if he knows. This is the number. It's in New Jersey." I gave her the number. "Okay, you got that?"

"Sure. What's the matter with you? You sound kind of weird. Did the sun get to you?"

"Yeah, the sun and everything else," I told her, stifling a yawn. "The five days since Grenada were sheer hell. Hardly had any sleep. Aaron is a maniac. He's giving up on the trip. That's why I want you to find Ken Helprin for me."

"But isn't he the guy who was seasick and grossed everyone out? What do you want him for?"

"Yeah, well... Maybe I find another boat short of crew. Ken might not even have a boat. That's what I want you to find out from Golden. It's Sunday evening. I don't know if this is his office or his home number. Please try, okay? I'll call you back in two hours. If you can't get in touch with him, please try again tomorrow. I'll be in touch. And, The Cat, thanks."

"No problem. Talk to you later." She hung up.

By now, everything was an effort. I walked back to the boat and thought I might be able to fall asleep.

Aaron sat in the cockpit with a young man. He introduced him to me. "This is Claudio. He wants to go to the States, so he is taking your place."

Claudio spoke little English. He was from Brazil. By way of his Portuguese and my Spanish, I was able to find out that he was an avid sailor. I felt a lot better about leaving the *PRI HA GOFEN* knowing that Aaron had crew.

I still had my bunk for the night and at long last, I was able to get a couple of hours of sleep.

When I awoke, it was dark and I was ravenous. I was not sure if I could still eat on board and did not want to get into an argument with Aaron.

Earlier, on the ferry dock, I had seen a guy with a basket, selling pretzels. I had to go to the phone booth anyway. The pretzel guy was no longer there, but I found an ice cream stand and bought a large parfait, vanilla ice cream with banana and whipped cream. I sat on a bench eating the delicious concoction and watched the people coming and going to and from the ferries that cross the harbor. Then I called The Cat.

"Hi, The Cat, did you get in touch with Mister Golden?"

"Yes, nice guy. He's single, wants to take me out. I am going to meet him tomorrow night on the Westside. Just kidding." She loved to tease me that way. "Listen, Ken Hellibelly or what's-his-name is in Cruz Bay. That's on St. John. Not St. Thomas. St. John. Write this down: he bought a boat, a trimaran; it's called the Happy Time Five. On the backstay is a flag with Snoopy on a surfboard. Did you write it down?"

"I don't have to write it down."

"Well, before you sounded a little out of it. Are you okay now? Your voice is better."

"Oh yes, I am fine. I already slept an hour or two. So, The Cat, that's great news. I'll try to get a flight out to Charlotte Amalie, St. Thomas tomorrow."

"Cruz Bay, St. John, Peter. What are you talking about, Charlotte and Amalie? Who are they? St. Thomas, Peter!"

"Don't be funny. This call is expensive. I am talking serious business here. There is a ferry from Charlotte Amalie to Cruz Bay. I have to find out more about that. Tomorrow morning I will take a taxi to the airport. Thanks, The Cat. You've been great."

*Man, this is turning out all right. Happy Time? Snoopy on a surfboard? Sounds good. I am in luck. Aaron, good-bye and good riddance!*

Aaron was not on board when I came back. I opened a jar of sandwich spread, helped myself to a bag of chips and, with a can of Red Stripe I had my evening meal in the cockpit.

To ensure a good night's sleep I drank another beer and went to bed before Aaron came back.

In the morning I packed my bags.

# HAPPY TIME V

Claudio arrived early in the morning of 23 April. All he carried was one large knapsack. It was a good thing that we had a language problem. He wanted to know why I was leaving the *PRI HA GOFEN*. Not knowing what he and Aaron might have been able to talk about, I was careful not to give the impression of being dissatisfied with the boat or her owner.

"I want to stay in the Caribbean," I said to him. He understood some of my Spanish. "The Virgin Islands are right here, only a twenty-minute flight away. Maybe I'll jump on another boat, do some sailing in the British and US Virgin Islands." Wishing him good luck and smooth sailing, I added, "She's a fine boat, comfortable and strong. Made for ocean cruising."

Then I picked up my duffel bag, slung my backpack over my shoulder and stepped ashore.

Aaron came out of his quarter berth. "You're leaving? Well good luck, sorry to see you go."

"Good-bye, Aaron. Have a safe trip," was all I managed to say.

I had a miserable time on the *PRI HA GOFEN*, and I was glad to leave. I looked forward to the change, although I did not have much of an idea what lay ahead of me. A new adventure, uncertain and exciting.

With my heavy duffel bag and the backpack, I walked the short distance to the ferry dock where always some taxis lined up.

"The airport," I said to the driver of the first car in line. He put my bags in the trunk of his Volvo, and we were off.

At the airport, I had no difficulty finding the counter of an airline that serviced the islands. I looked for signs like *Virgin Air, Air Caribbean*—anything like that.

On the wall behind one counter, I read: *Antigua via Charlotte Amalie. Next departure 10:45.* I was right on time and bought a ticket. Ten minutes later I sat in a twin-engine turbo-prop for the short trip to the capital of the US Virgin Islands.

This was getting exciting now. I was in quest of the trimaran *HAPPY TIME V,* captain Kenneth Helprin. Golden had told The Cat where I would find him, but how old was that information? Ken could be anywhere by now. The boat, the trimaran, how big was it? I did not think Ken had a lot of money. How new, how old, how seaworthy or decrepit, how well or poorly maintained might the *HAPPY TIME* be?

Then a thought occurred to me: what if Ken already had crew? *Oh boy, what am I doing? I am homeless. Not the New York City variety of homeless, but a bum just the same.*

The plane took off. I had a beautiful view of the islands spread out over the blue sea beneath the wings. Minutes later, the landing gear bumped lightly on the runway of Charlotte Amalie airport. That was the first leg of my new adventure.

Now I had to get to Cruz Bay, St. John where I would find the *HAPPY TIME V*. Outside the terminal a dispatcher directed a host of passengers from various flights to waiting taxis.

"How do I get to St. John?" I asked.

"You take a taxi to the center of town, then a bus to Red Hook. There you get on the ferry for Cruz Bay."

All right. Taxi, bus, ferry.

St. John is the small island just to the east of St. Thomas. Farther south is St. Croix. Beside these three islands, there is a myriad of small islets, many of them uninhabited.

The taxi dropped me off in the colorful center of town. There was the old market square with the auction hall, trading post for slaves only a century and a half ago. Nowadays, men and women offer vegetables, fruit and flowers for sale, as well as straw hats, multi-colored scarves, incense, perfumed candles and, under the tables, ganja (marijuana) and who knows what else.

Shoppers, from island folk and Rastafarians to tourists, moved among the tables set up for business. Men, young and old, sat on crates, playing Dominoes.

Steeldrum music blared from speakers at one corner of the square. At another corner I saw a couple of safari buses, already crowded with passengers, on the roofs crates, bundles and baskets.

"Red Hook?" I asked. No, it wasn't one of these. "Red Hook? None of these are going to Red Hook?"

At last somebody knew. "Wait right here, mon. Two-thirty, maybe, if he show up. I'd take taxi, if I was you, mon. Bus, you never know." Then, in a slightly lower voice, "You want ganja? I got the good stuff."

"No, thanks, I just wait for the bus."

The bright blue and yellow safari buses have open bench seating. Beside the driver, a guy on each bus yells out the destination or something I can't understand. He is the one who later collects the fare. One of those "conductors" who seemed a little more trustworthy, confirmed that a bus to Red Hook should be coming shortly. I put down my heavy load by the curb and waited.

Eventually, a bus appeared that even had a hand-written sign *Red Hook* taped to the windshield. People scrambled on board. I got a seat in the last row, with just enough room for my two bags. Under loud screaming between those on the bus and those left behind, we moved away from the curb.

Pedestrians, motorbikes and bicycles crowded the narrow streets of downtown Charlotte Amalie. The driver tried to mow them all down, but failed.

At last we were on a wide thoroughfare. Large buildings—shipping companies, banks, insurance companies—on our left; the harbor close at hand to the right. I saw some small freighters and tankers, passenger ferries and, on the far side, two huge cruise ships.

We came to what seemed to be the yacht haven and a modern high-rise hotel. In the anchorage there must have been a hundred boats. On one small boat, a trimaran, very close to the shore, I read the name *HAPPY TIME V*.

*HAPPY TIME V? What? Is that... it must be! There's Snoopy on a surfboard!* "Hey, stop the bus! Let me off here." People all around me looked at me as if I were a mad man. *I'm the only white guy on the bus and acting like crazy.* The bus pulled to the curb and stopped.

The conductor came around. "What you doin', mon? You sick?"

"What do I owe you?" I dragged my baggage past the feet of the people in my row. "No, I'm not sick. There's my boat. I've got to get off here. What do I owe you?"

"I dunno, mon. Short ride. Gimme fifty cents."

"Thanks for stopping." I put my bags on the ground and reached in my pocket. "Here's a dollar. Thanks again."

I picked up my duffel bag and my knapsack, and started down the embankment.

"Your change, mon!" I heard behind me.

The embankment from the highway down to the narrow, gravelly beach was steep. I yelled, "Happy Time, Happy Time?" and waved my arms.

Ken sat in the cockpit. There was someone with him. A woman, with long blonde hair. *Oh no, this not good, not good at all. How can I intrude in that?*

Ken heard me and turned around to see who was calling out to him. He got up and into the dinghy tied to the boat's stern. Rowing with his back to me, he did not know who I was until he reached the beach.

"Hey, Ken, you won't believe how I found you. Long story."

"I want to hear all about it," he said. "Want to come on board? Here, hand me that bag. I was expecting the compass adjuster; thought it was he calling from the beach."

"I left Aaron in San Juan. I need a place to stay. Actually, I am looking for a berth on a boat. I see, you already have crew."

I got into the dinghy and Ken rowed us back to his boat. "Well, Jeff Darren is with me, a young fellow I met in Cruz Bay. We'll see what we can work out."

Exactly seven hours after leaving the *PRI HA GOFEN* at San Juan, I stepped on board the *HAPPY TIME* in the harbor of Charlotte Amalie. Jeff reached over the side and pulled my bags on board. He had long blond hair. *Okay, not a woman. That's a relief.*

Ken introduced us. "Jeff, this is Peter. He might be joining us for a while. We will talk about that."

Ken's deep, calm voice was pleasant and comforting to hear, but I could not help feeling like an intruder, as if I were forcing them to take me on against their will.

"Jeff, good to meet you." We shook hands. "Listen," I turned to Ken. "Please, don't feel obligated. You asked me once to join you on a boat you were going to buy. I chose to go with Aaron. Now, here I am. All those boats around here... I am sure some of them are short on crew."

A call from land interrupted us. "That's the compass adjuster. I have to go and get him." Ken rowed the short distance to the beach and came back with a man who made a few adjustments to the compass and prepared a deviation card—a list of degrees to be added or subtracted from the compass readings to arrive at the correct heading.

Jeff took the man back to shore, while Ken started to raise the anchor. I felt a little useless for a moment, a normal feeling on a boat before things become familiar.

As soon as Jeff returned, Ken hand-cranked the one-cylinder Diesel engine and we were underway. "We anchor at Buck Island for the night," he announced. Tomorrow morning we sail to Cruz Bay." He took the tiller and steered us out of the harbor. "Buck Island is just a mile or two south of here."

The little old Diesel hammered away, a sound that reminded me of the fishing boats on my Baltic Sea. I sat back and looked around. It was my first time on a trimaran.

My duffel bag and backpack were still in the cockpit, where Jeff had put them. A glance down the companionway left me in mild horror. Dirty dishes, pots and pans on the two-burner kerosene stove and in the sink next to it. A table, folded down, to allow two people to pass each other in the narrow cabin. A short settee opposite the galley.

On each side of the cabin was a crawl space, not more than three feet high. An open hatch forward served as the only source of light. A fixed wooden roof over the companionway and the cockpit provided shelter, but prevented light from getting below. Transparent plastic sheets, when rolled down from the roof on both sides to enclose the cockpit, formed what some sailors call the doghouse.

The wide beam of a trimaran does not contribute to interior space. From each side of the narrow center hull, wings extend to the sponsons, which are basically nothing more than outriggers, lending stability to the craft. While looking rather clumsy, sailboats of this type are very fast, owing to their narrow hulls, minimal draft and ability to remain upright, or nearly so, even in strong winds.

We anchored in the lee of Buck Island, a mere rock covered with lush, green vegetation.

"Jeff is very good in the galley," Ken praised his young shipmate. "He can whip up a pretty good meal. We have Pork & Beans, Dinty Moore stew, corned beef and tuna. Jeff sometimes adds ketchup, mustard or mayonnaise. Makes a pretty tasty dish."

That's it? I thought. *From Bulgar to beans...* I kept my thoughts to myself.

"Sounds all right," I said. "On the PRI HA GOFEN I had to eat Bulgar."

"Well, first of all let us welcome you on board. You like Bloody Marys?"

Ken got up, shook some ketchup into a pitcher, added Worcestershire Sauce and Tabasco, and then poured vodka into the mixture. From a blue plastic jug he filled the pitcher with water and stirred with a wooden spoon. Jeff brought plastic glasses and we toasted each other with lukewarm Bloody Marys á la *HAPPY TIME*.

"I bought this boat ten days ago," Ken told me. "She is nineteen years old. The previous owner built her in his backyard, somewhere in California. He and his wife sailed her across the Pacific to Hawaii, then to Tahiti and

Indonesia. There they stayed for many years. That's where they added the doghouse. See the exquisite carving on this wood?" Ken pointed to the posts supporting the roof. I saw some grotesque shapes carved into the bleached teak. "They sailed through the Indian Ocean, rounded Cape of Good Hope and then crossed the Atlantic to Brazil. They spent years in Fortaleza, Recife and Bahia, always living on the boat. The last couple of years they lived in these islands."

Ken spoke with great affection of the boat and the people who had built it and made it their home for so many years. He did not say how much he paid for the boat and I did not ask. After a while he continued, "she is only twenty-eight feet long, but with a beam of sixteen, there is plenty of room."

I thought, where? Where is all that room?

"I have the starboard wing for my sleeping quarters, Jeff is on port. He was here first, so he keeps his bunk. We set you up in the cockpit. I have these boards to extend the seat to a double bunk."

"That's fine with me. When it rains I can let down the plastic side curtains. I have a sleeping bag, so I'll be okay." Under no circumstances would I sleep in one of those wings. I would suffocate.

I could not imagine myself on this boat for any length of time. The living conditions were primitive, there was no sense of order, everything was haphazard. The dirty dishes, the water jugs, the food situation, the sanitation… Where, for instance, was the head? What about hygiene?

I got the feeling that Aaron was right. Ken had no sense of orderliness and cleanliness. Then there was this archaic one-cylinder Diesel with the hand crank. The boat had no *Loran* and no SatNav. Was there any safety equipment? In what conditions were the sails? Was there a plan of any kind?

42

After a while Ken said, "This boat has made it three quarters around the world. She can do it again."

*He wants to sail around the world in this contraption? Is he looking for an epitaph: Lost at Sea?*

Seriously he said, "Jeff and I talked about sailing over to St. Maarten and then south along the chain of islands. Eventually to Panama and into the Pacific."

Although he still reminded me of Don Quixote, he now took on more the image of a pirate. Only the wooden leg and an eye patch were missing. Don Quixote fought windmills and imaginary armies on his Rosinante. Kenneth Helprin chased islands in the sky.

I said, "Let's take it one day at a time."

Meanwhile I was starving, but my appetite was at minus one, on a scale from one to ten. Jeff produced celery stalks and cut some carrots into strips. Then he opened a can of corned beef. That was our evening meal. We had more Bloody Marys.

Night had fallen and Ken lit a kerosene stable lantern. I told them about my voyage with Aaron. "He really turned out to be an intolerable individual," I said and ended my story talking about how he treated Sylvia. "What a miserable character, and she so fine and articulate. I really liked her. She is an extraordinary woman."

"She is a speech therapist. Did you know that? A very intelligent lady. He, on the other hand, is a peasant, no manners and no social skills," said Ken.

"That's for sure. I liked to listen to her, but I think he is frustrated because he burdened himself with her; the cripple, I mean."

Ken, the psychologist, was the expert. "Well, you are right. Of course, it is more complicated than that, not quite so simple."

In my mind, I compared Aaron Orbin and Ken Helprin. The *PRI HA GOFEN* was clean, orderly and comfortable, but Aaron was intolerable. On the *HAPPY TIME,* conditions were intolerable, but Ken was a friend— and a dreamer, a romantic.

Jeff brought out a deck of cards and we played for a while under the kerosene lamp in the cockpit. Then Ken picked up his guitar and strummed a few chords. Jeff said good night, went to brush his teeth on the foredeck and then crept into his claustrophobic berth. Ken showed me how to fix the boards to widen my bunk and then he too went to bed.

I rolled out my sleeping bag and was glad to be able to lie down. The tropical night air, the sound of the waves hitting the rocks at Buck Island, the lights from Charlotte Amalie in the distance… all that contributed to a peaceful sleep.

The sail to St. John, in a steady easterly breeze, took three hours. We anchored in the harbor of Cruz Bay and I felt the calm, relaxed atmosphere of this island from the moment we arrived.

I fell in love with Cruz Bay as soon as we rowed ashore. In contrast to Charlotte Amalie, there were no dirty market place, no screaming vendors, no yelling bus conductors; no multitudes jamming narrow streets and no tourists hunting for bargains in duty-free shops. Everything and everyone seemed to move at a slower pace.

The dock where the ferries from Red Hook landed jutted out from a small park with palm trees, walkways and benches. Behind the park were an ice-cream parlor and a souvenir shop selling postcards, film and T-shirts. To one side was a delicatessen and next to it a kiosk that sold magazines and lottery tickets. A couple of taxis stood at the curb, their drivers sitting on a park bench nearby.

Ken, Jeff and I crossed the park and walked past the Customs and Immigration building, the doctor's office and the post office. Local people were hanging out in a little open-sided shack at a corner. We sat down on stools at the counter and ordered chicken thighs. This place sold nothing but chicken thighs and drumsticks, but a great variety of drinks was available. I ordered a Heineken.

Kenneth Helprin, quite the hippy-type left over from the sixties, and Jeff Darren, eighteen-year old, longhaired hillbilly, made a strange pair. Ken's olive bellbottom pants and brass buckle belt were as outdated as Jeff's gym shorts were avant-gardes. When I joined them, we made an even stranger threesome. My khaki shorts and T-shirt were far too new and touristy, my beard not yet long enough to be called that. As the "normal" one, I was he odd man out.

We left the chicken shack and walked along the road that passed Mongoose Junction. There were fashionable shops selling beach wear, accessories and souvenirs, a fine restaurant with outdoor seating in a tropical garden, and a bakery.

Turning a corner, a street led up a steep hill. To my surprise, there was a regular supermarket. Near the top of the hill we came to a bungalow. Ken knocked at the door. "Friends of mine," he explained to me.

We entered a low cottage and walked through to a small patio, separated from the neighbors by a high hedge. Ken's friends were a much younger couple. Their unruly kid was banging incessantly on the lid of the barbecue grill.

"Good to see you, Ken. How did it go? Jeff, how you doin'?" The husband shook hands with both of them. Then he looked at me.

"Hey, good to be back. This is Peter," Ken introduced me as an old friend from New York. "He joined us yesterday in St. Thomas. Peter has been a sailor all his life."

The couple welcomed me into their home. "A friend of Ken's is a friend of our's," said the wife who came into the patio with a pitcher and glasses. "Wine cooler!

Welcome back, Ken, Jeff. Hi, Peter. Make yourselves at home. Brad, stop it!"

I am sorry I don't know the names of these friendly people. Either I never knew, or I forgot. But I do remember the name of the five or six year-old boy. It's Brad Stopit. I also remember that Brad never stopped it.

I didn't quite find out how these regular, urban people came to live on St. John and by what rare intervention they were friends with Kenneth Helprin. Somehow I gathered that they knew each other on a scholarly basis, either as colleagues or a professor-student relation. Seeking a more relaxed lifestyle, I guess, the couple had chosen Cruz Bay as their home.

"We are almost ready," Ken said. "I picked up the EPIRB (Emergency Position Indicating Radio Beacon) in Charlotte Amalie and ordered the head. I'll get that in a couple of days. I also bought some Stop-Rot, a liquid wood preservative. We'll treat the plywood of the sponsons with that. Then we only have to stock up on provisions."

I don't think our hosts had any idea what Ken was talking about. Anyway, neither their comments nor their facial expressions conveyed any encouragement or confidence. Polite or doubtful nodding and gestures were the only reaction I observed.

When I heard Ken say *Stop-Rot*, I almost cringed. If there were any dry rot in the boat, it would be too late for a preservative. That stuff is good only for prevention, not as a cure.

On our way back to the dinghy Ken took me aside. "I have had a little talk with Jeff. He agrees with me to take you on board. He likes you and you are certainly a valuable asset in our upcoming adventure. So, I welcome you as a member of the crew of the HAPPY TIME V." He held out his hand and I took it.

I realized I had just committed myself. "Ken, I'll be happy to sail with you. My concern is the boat. Home-built, nineteen years old. Have you discovered any dry rot? Or any other weak spots, for that matter?"

"Nothing serious. Only in the sponsons. Stop-Rot will take care of that. In Roadtown we will examine the rigging. I know a rigger there. Then we'll be set. As I said, the boat has done it before; she can do it again."

I felt uncertain about that, but I did not know how to get myself out of this tight spot. I liked Ken, a naïve dreamer, an idealist, a romantic adventurer. He was an incurable optimist. Reality eluded him. I knew I would stick with him, but I also knew that I shouldn't.

Jeff Darren has never been anywhere near boats. His parents treated him after his graduation from high school to a vacation in the Virgin Islands. For the first time out of his rural Vermont, he savored the so different life in these islands. A dormant sense of freedom and adventure awoke in him and he decided to stay in the islands.

He met Ken, the old seafarer, and he trusted him. A bond developed, and Jeff felt safe with this kind, understanding, benevolent man.

Indeed, Ken was all that, but he was also irresponsible. His haphazard way of venturing out upon the ocean with an old, ill-equipped boat was reckless. He did not see it that way, or did not want to see it. The ocean is no place to fool around. The ocean can kill.

For the next few days we remained at anchor in the cozy harbor of Cruz Bay. I had discovered a rustic restaurant that had a bathhouse, a bamboo shack, in the backyard. A fifty-five gallon drum on a high rack dispensed water through a showerhead. For a dollar or two, the proprietress let the water run for five minutes.

Several times I used this facility and had lunch or dinner at the restaurant, alone or with Ken and Jeff.

There was no movie house in Cruz Bay, but once or twice a week a film was shown in a sort of assembly hall. One evening, sitting on wooden benches without backrests, we saw *The Bridge on the River Kwai.*

Ken and Jeff went by ferry across to Red Hook to pick up the new head. During their absence, I equipped myself with the can of *Stop-Rot*, putty and putty knife and, with a flashlight, slithered through the wing into the starboard sponson.

There was dry rot, all right. In some places the plywood had buckled. With fiberglass putty and resin, I repaired the worst spots and treated the entire length of the sponson with a coat of the strong smelling liquid preservative.

After an hour of trying not to suffocate, I repeated the procedure on the port side. Here I found no dry rot and applied only a coat of Stop-Rot, but I did not think that it would do any good.

On the day before leaving Cruz Bay, Ken and Jeff installed the new head. I was glad not to get involved in that messy job.

The three of us went to take our showers at the bathhouse and then went to Ken's friends for a farewell party. Ken and Jeff brought a gallon jug of Burgundy; I had found a toy drum in the souvenir shop for Brad Stopit.

There were chicken and sausages on the grill, a big bowl with a green salad, and potato salad from the deli on the table. Brad didn't stop it on the drum. He would have preferred the lid of the grill, but it was too hot from the cooking.

The evening went by quickly with talking, eating, drinking and laughing. At midnight we said our good-byes and farewells, and went back to the boat. The drumming continued in my head throughout the night.

In the morning I had time to go to the bakery at Mongoose Junction to buy three loaves of French bead, still warm, just out of the oven.

On my return, we stowed the dinghy on the foredeck and Jeff pulled up the anchor. Ken got the Diesel going and slowly we chugged out of the harbor of Cruz Bay.

We were underway. The trade winds were blowing moderately. It was a great day to start our voyage. I believe it was April 29 or 30.

Ken pushed two sail bags out through the forward hatch and I hanked the jib onto the forestay. Both the jib and the mainsail were in fair condition.

Jeff was at the tiller; Ken hoisted the main and then killed the engine. The trimaran picked up speed. We were sailing.

The speed log did not work. "Let's see what's wrong with it," said Ken calmly. "There is a fine beach at Lovango, the low island over there. We can drive the boat up to the beach, get into the water and check it out."

Lovango is an uninhabited little island and Ken explained how it got its name. "There used to be a whorehouse. The sailors who stopped there called it Love an' go."

"But are there still any women today?" asked Jeff.

"Sorry, Jeff," said Ken, "that's a long time ago."

"Then why go?" I asked. "Oh right, to check out the speed log and go for a swim."

The trimaran slid smoothly onto the beach. In an instant the three of us were in the clear, refreshing water. The impeller near the bow of the center hull, just below the waterline, was completely corroded. Ken pulled it out of its housing. "Well, no big deal. We just have to sail without it."

49

We pushed the boat off the beach, and once again we were underway.

Along the north shore of St. John, we fought against a strong east wind until we passed Thatch Island. Then, in Sir Francis Drake Channel, we tacked twice to reach the harbor of Roadtown on the island of Tortola, the capital of the British Virgin Islands. In this town, smaller than Charlotte Amalie, the cruising sailor can find everything needed to outfit his boat. There are charter companies, ship chandlers and yachting services. The harbor is spacious and exposed only to weather from the south.

The shallow draft of the trimaran allowed us to anchor close to the shore. This was convenient for us, for we stayed at this port longer than anticipated. Ken had contracted a rigger, but he was not available until two days after our arrival. We had discovered some rust stains on the shrouds, and the turnbuckles were probably as old as the boat.

The man came out to us in his dinghy and looked at the rigging. He was skeptical from the moment he stepped on board. "I recommend to replace the whole thing, stays, shrouds and turnbuckles," he said to Ken. "They are all weak and will certainly fail the first time there is any real pressure on the sails." He quoted a price, which I don't recall, for I have lost all my notes.

Ken's disappointment showed in his ashen face. It was as if the verdict had touched his pride. He thought so highly of his boat.

"What do you think, Pete," he asked me. He was the only one I allowed to call me Pete. Perhaps he was hoping that I disagreed with the rigger, but I thought, sailing all the way into the Pacific with shoddy rigging?

"Ken," I said, "the wire is old and tired. It is not stainless. There is rust, and the turnbuckles show signs of wear. I think he is right. You see that, don't you?"

"It's a matter of cost."

"No, Ken," I objected, "it's a matter of safety."

"Yes, it is a matter of safety for all three of us. Are you willing to split the cost? Say, we split it three ways." He turned to Jeff. "What do you say, Jeff?"

Jeff shook his head. "Well, I don't really have any money. I have enough for food and stuff, but that's about it. I don't think my parents would chip in on that."

"Pete, I realize we need new rigging. We go half and half, okay?"

"I'll tell you what, Ken. Since there are three of us, I'll pay my third. The other two thirds, that's up to you."

And that is what we agreed on.

The following day the rigger showed up with spools of stainless steel wire and turnbuckles, and replaced all the standing rigging. Hoisted in the bosun's chair, he removed the old shrouds and stays at the masthead and replaced them with new wire. Back down on deck, he cut them into the right length and swaged on the turnbuckles.

"Now for the fine tuning," he addressed Ken. "Some people like their rigging tight and unforgiving. Others prefer some degree of slack to allow the mast to adjust to wind conditions and points of sailing."

"Oh, I certainly want it tight," Ken answered.

I totally disagreed. A tight rigging puts a lot of pressure on the mast, pulling it down. But I kept quiet. *It's his boat.*

The mast of the *HAPPY TIME V* was deck-stepped, meaning it stood on the cabin roof. A two-by-four, mounted on the keel, supported the roof directly under the foot of the mast.

The rigger adjusted the turnbuckles. Ken tested the shrouds that were as tight as guitar strings. Our mast stood proudly pointing skyward.

With the money in his pocket, the man wished us safe passage, pulled the starter cord of his outboard and went back to shore.

Jeff was essentially the cook on board. Together we convinced Ken to buy some "real" food. "What about meat, Ken? Potatoes, rice, pasta? We don't think we can live on Pork & Beans, ketchup and mayonnaise," we argued.

"And, Ken, please, let us get a case or two of beer," I added.

We stocked up and had almost decent provisions on board. We carried water in two ten-gallon jugs, tied to the handrails along the cabin roof. Four additional five-gallon Jerry cans completed our water supply. *Forty gallons for a crew of three? What will we do in the Pacific, with a thousand miles between islands?*

Ken, the optimist, saw no such problems. "There is plenty of rain. That's what these hoses from the doghouse roof are for. They attach like this at the corners here and run into the Jerry cans." He showed me his clever invention. "We will never be without fresh water."

*What are we? Explorers in the twelfth century?*

On May 6—I believe it was May 6—we sailed out of Roadtown. Several tacks in Sir Francis Drake Channel against the strong easterly trade winds put stress on the boat and the rigging. *HAPPY TIME V* behaved well and we gained confidence. *Snoopy* followed along on his surfboard.

At The Baths on the south end of Virgin Gorda we marveled at the boulders the size of houses. These enormous, gray shapes, reminding of gigantic elephants, remain to this day an unexplained phenomenon. Leaving *HAPPY TIME* at anchor, we swam ashore and explored the rocks, the passages and hollows between them and the cavities filled with sun-heated water, which gave this place its name: The Baths.

Late afternoon we arrived at Spanish Harbour on Virgin Gorda and docked at the head of a pier in the Yacht Haven. From here we planned our departure for the Lesser Antilles, or the Windward Islands. I have never been sure about this designation. Lesser? Where are the Majors? Windward and Leeward? Anyway, the chain of islands extends from Cuba, Hispaniola and Puerto Rico eastward to the Virgin Islands, and then curves toward the south and ends with Grenada.

We spent a full day at leisure at the Spanish Harbour Yacht Haven. I wrote letters and postcards. In Cruz Bay I had several rolls of film developed. My Minolta took pretty good photos and I had interesting ones of Martinique, Cariacou and Grenada. I sorted the pictures and mailed a few in a letter to Julia, others I sent to The Cat. For some reason, none of them ever reached their destinations. The roll with photos of St. John and The Baths was still in the camera. Those, too, no one ever saw.

When we sailed out of the Yacht Haven in the morning of the following day, we headed north toward Necker Island. From there we could expect a good angle on the wind for the twenty-four hour crossing to St. Maarten.

Solitary and lush, Necker Island is a verdant rock with a beautiful beach. Located south of the low island of Anegada, it is a god jumping-off point to all of the Lesser Antilles. That day we had a favorable wind, blowing fifteen knots from slightly north of east.

We stopped briefly at Necker Island to drill a few screws into a beam of the cabin roof. The wooden beam showed a foot-long split in the center. Ken was content with the superficial repair; I, however, became suspicious of what caused the crack.

We began our cruise across the Anegada Passage in late afternoon. Close-hauled, to make good a course directly for St. Maarten, the boat labored in the four to five-foot seas.

In the evening, Jeff reported more water in the bilge than there had previously been. Ken took the hand pump from the lazaret in the cockpit and handed it to Jeff.

"Here, Jeff. Give it a few strokes. No big deal."

Jeff was a quiet guy. He always did what he was asked to do and never showed ill will. The hose on the pump was not long enough to reach overboard. Jeff had to pump the water into a bucket, which I then emptied over the side. This went on for a while. Ken pointed the flashlight to the ceiling beam. The crack had opened again, wider than before we had put in the screws. I was at the tiller, while Jeff pumped and Ken had the first heaves of seasickness.

During the night nothing noteworthy happened. I remained at the tiller, Jeff periodically pumped and Ken went to lie down in his bunk. He took with him one of the pots from the galley. I resolved never to eat anything cooked on this boat from then on.

The wind continued east at about fifteen knots, the sea at four to five feet. Our compass heading was 135 degrees, or southeast. I spread out the chart and, by the flashlight, tried to determine our position. Since the log was out of commission, I had to estimate our speed. At midnight, I calculated: eight hours at seven knots puts us at a distance of fifty-six nautical miles southeast of Necker Island.

I called Ken. "This is where we are, approximately. Give or take a few miles for leeway. Come, take a look."

"I take your word for it, Pete." He did not move from his bunk, retching into the pot.

Most of the time, when he wasn't pumping, Jeff stood next to me at the tiller. The night air was mild,

*HAPPY TIME* moving along with the even rise and fall of the long ocean swells.

Toward morning Jeff reported, "The bilge fills almost as fast as I can pump. What do you think is wrong?"

I knew what was wrong, but did not exactly tell him. "In St. Maarten we will have to give very serious consideration to the continuation of this voyage." I added, "if we make it to St. Maarten. Can you find us a candy bar or something? We haven't eaten anything since… I don't remember when?"

Jeff came up the companionway with two Milky Ways. "The water is now above the floor boards. I'd better go back down and pump. I'll also use the big steamer pot. That way I can keep pumping while you empty out the bucket. You think that's okay with Ken?"

"At this point it doesn't matter anymore whether it's okay with him. What matters is to stay afloat." In my view, we were just biding time.

I estimated our speed was down to three or four knots and we could no longer hold our course. The boat did not point as well as it did before, meaning we had to fall off the wind, unable to head for St. Maarten. Perhaps we can reach Eustatius or St. Barts, I figured in my head, but that would add at least a couple of hours. We had hoped to reach St. Maarten by seven o'clock, but that was now out of the question. If, *IF*, we could get as far as Eustatius or St. Barts, it would not be before midnight.

"You mean, we can't go to St. Maarten?" asked Jeff.

"Not unless we tack, and that I would not dare with the boat in the condition she's in. Any shifting of pressure could break her up."

I did not even think of asking Ken. He was completely uninterested, in a state where nothing mattered to him. His will had left him. Severe seasickness can have such an effect on a person. I was in charge, and I thought only of survival.

By noon, pumping could no longer keep up with the water coming in. At three in the afternoon I estimated the Dutch island of Saba, the nearest land, at about thirty miles north of our position—eight or ten hours away. To reach Saba, we would have to tack. I rejected that idea for fear of sinking the boat in the process.

*We won't make it, we won't make it. Speed down to two knots. I have to get Ken out. If we sink, he will drown in his bunk. If necessary, we have to drag him out.*

"Jeff, where's the EPIRB? I want it here next to me," I said causally, not to alarm him. "And, Jeff, get your life jacket, just in case. Get mine, too. Do you know where Ken keeps his?"

"I'll get it," said Jeff.

He went below and came back with the EPIRB and our life jackets. Jeff went down again and found Ken standing by the VHF, ankle-deep in water, speaking into the mike.

I saw a chance to bring him out into the cockpit, when I heard the reply coming over the radio. "This is Rescue Station Saba. What is your emergency? Over."

Ken spoke hesitantly, in his low voice, "We are taking on water and need an extra pump. Over."

"We will send someone out to you. What is your position? Over."

*Has he lost his senses? A pump?* In one leap, I was next to Ken and grabbed the mike from his shaking hand.

"Mayday, Mayday, Mayday. HAPPY TIME V sinking. Position Anegada Passage, approximately thirty miles south of Saba. Three persons on board…"

The beam over our heads broke. Wood splintered. The ceiling caved in. The mast came crashing down. The two-by-four disappeared through the bottom. We stood to

56

our hips in water. The radio was dead. It was exactly four o'clock in the afternoon of May 9, 1985.

Ken's voice came trembling, incredulous. "Oh no, oh no! What happened?"

The three of us stood next to the mast that stuck in an angle through the ceiling, its foot jammed into the floorboards.

I scrambled out the companionway and activated the EPIRB, which I had left in the cockpit. The floorboards here too were under water. The boat remained stable, floating on the sponsons.

Jeff came out. "Ken wants to go back into his bunk, which is only two inches above the water."

"He is crazy. You have to get him out here. He's delirious."

"He won't come. He says he's safe there."

"How can we get him out of that crawl space? For now, the boat remains afloat on the sponsons, but for how long? We are lucky the sea is as calm as it is. The heavy engine will pull us down with the first irregular wave."

Jeff and I put on our PFDs (Coast Guard lingo for Personal Floatation Device). My duffel bag was under water in the forward storage area, but I could reach my backpack in the lazaret. From it, I removed my wallet with credit cards and my passport, and put them in the waterproof pocket of my foul weather jacket, which I wore over my PFD. Jeff said, he also had his passport on him.

I stepped into my yellow rubber sea boots. Jeff was barefoot.

"You think our Mayday got through?" Jeff asked me.

"Yeah, maybe those were the last words they heard."

We both stood on top of the lazaret behind the tiller, resting our elbows on the roof of the doghouse. I held the EPIRB.

"It's now up to this thing. It alerts aircraft and ground stations via satellites."

"How fast can a rescue boat from Saba be here?"

"Who knows? Two, three hours. If they have a boat capable of eighteen knots. Not before six or seven tonight."

I asked Jeff to help me get the dinghy into the water. We worked well together. Not even for a moment was there any panic. On the foredeck, barely above water, we untied the dinghy and flipped it overboard. I tied it to the port side of the main hull, near the stern.

"Jeff, put two of the five-gallon jugs in it."

I assessed the situation as follows: the constant pressure of the mast on the two-by-four supporting the mast had gradually opened the seams on the bottom of the hull. For that reason we took on water long before disaster struck. The excessive tightening of the rigging was a contributing factor, but eventually the hull would have given way. The keel broke loose and left a gaping hole under the floorboards. I believed we could stay afloat indefinitely. The sponsons gave enough buoyancy — provided the state of the sea remained as calm as it was.

The waiting began. Jeff and I talked calmly. Besides his clothing, he had few belongings and no valuables. Most of what I owned was in my duffel bag in the forepeak: clothes and shoes, my binoculars, pictures, a watch, documents, nautical books and a sextant. Waterlogged and heavy, it was impossible to retrieve and drag it past the mast, which barred the way. My knapsack in the lazaret was now also under water.

Ken remained in his bunk. Jeff and I were determined to drag him out by force, if that should become necessary. So far sea conditions were calm enough to keep the *HAPPY TIME V* afloat.

As daylight faded, we observed a light low above the horizon where the sun had just set. This light, heading directly toward us, seemed to come from far away. As it came closer, we recognized it as a jet of the US Coast Guard.

We waved to the plane as it passed over us. It made a wide turn and came back. For the next ten minutes, the aircraft crossed our position eight times from various directions and dropped three smoke flares, a triangle, with us in the center.

The jet disappeared, the flares burned out and we could do no more than wait. They had spotted us and that gave us a great deal of confidence, but we still could not motivate Ken to come out of his bunk.

Long after dark we saw a faint light on the horizon. "Jeff, get me the binoculars from Ken's locker, and tell him the rescue boat is coming. We have to be ready to abandon ship."

Through the binoculars I saw a ship approaching, but was it the rescue boat? It could be any vessel.

I found the big flashlight in the lazaret and began to signal SOS, three short, three long, three short flashes. Ken came out and sat in a corner of the doghouse, shivering. Every few minutes he had the dry heaves—a miserable picture. Jeff helped him into his life jacket.

Jeff joined me again and stood next to me on the lazaret. I kept signaling SOS, slowly, as the flashlight had no quick release button. I did not know how far it might be visible. A rescue boat would home in on the EPIRB, but freighters did not usually receive EPIRB signals.

At a quarter past nine, Jeff and I saw it was a huge freighter coming toward us. The big vessel dimmed her lights twice. "They saw us, they saw us!"

We discerned the bow pointing directly at us, the black hull rising high out of the water, slowly closing in on us. We waved frantically and went forward on the port side. *How can we climb up there? Are they coming down to get us?*

Still the ship kept coming, her steep bow already above us. "Stop!" we yelled at the terrifying black shape. Attempting to fend off, we balanced on the port sponson.

Although hardly moving, the freighter's bow hit the sponson hard enough to knock off the forward two feet. The rest of the sponson immediately filled with water and went down. Jeff and I scrambled onto the center hull. Ken was still in his corner of the cockpit.

Slowly, silently the full length of the ship slid past us. *They aren't going to leave us here?* What was left of the *HAPPY TIME V* was now barely hanging on the starboard sponson, center hull completely flooded. The boat could go down any moment. We scrambled onto the roof of the doghouse. Ken found the energy to step on top of the cabin and then joined us on the slanted roof.

The big vessel needed half an hour to maneuver back into position next to us. A pilot ladder hung down its side. Jeff grabbed the ladder and started to climb. Ken, standing in front of me, had to get up before I could reach for one of the rungs. When he was out of the way, I was able to get hold of the lowest step. Hanging on with both hands, I slid off the roof into the water and began my ascent on the vertical wall of the hull.

In these hectic moments I had not noticed the arrival of a helicopter, which hovered above and brightly illuminated the scene. Clambering up the wooden rungs of the rope ladder required all my attention.

When I reached the top, Ken and Jeff were already standing on deck. Smiling, laughing Chinese men dragged me over the bulwark, scraping my knees and shins.

I looked over the side and saw nothing of the wreck of the *HAPPY TIME V.*

I think, the three of us were a little befuddled, not yet quite aware of what had happened in these last few minutes.

Someone escorted us to the captain's quarters. At the door, before entering, I took off my boots, which were full of water and left them outside. I remember the young Chinese officer smiling compassionately. "Is okay," he said.

In the room was a desk with a computer and a lot of other electronic devices on it. There were comfortable chairs and a round coffee table. The captain stood up and greeted us cordially with handshakes. He seemed to me a very young man to be in charge of such a large vessel.

"Welcome on board the PACIFIC FREEDOM," he smiled and invited us to sit down.

# Life on the
# PACIFIC FREEDOM

Captain Henry Eng ordered the steward to serve sandwiches and tea. The radio officer came in and asked for one of the survivors to talk to the chopper pilot. Ken designated Jeff to do the honors.

The captain was in his mid-thirties. He spoke marginal English. We gave him a brief report of our ordeal. Jeff came back and said the helicopter pilot needed to hear from one of the survivors directly that all three POB (persons on board) were safe and unhurt.

The first officer entered and spoke to the captain. I guessed he reported the end of the operation. The following is part of the Master Statement of which I later received a copy:

2115 2nd Mate found "SOS" flash signal on starboard bow reporting to captain.
2120 R.S.B.E. ordered changing Diesel for Maneuvering and crew on Man over boat drill station.
2125 Reduced speed, crew were mustered

on station.
2130 The yacht was drifting from port bow
to astern.
2150 Rigged pilot ladder and life boat No. 1
swung out and lower to accommodation
deck.
2200 Approached to yacht and in a distance.
2203 Survivors picked up.
2205 Yacht drifting away, ordered to use
Fuel for sea speed.
2210 Stowed pilot ladder in and Life boat
was in position.
2212 Speed was up then R.F.A.
Detention from 2115 hrs to 2212 hrs, total
time used 57 minutes and fuel consumed 0.5
M/T of diesel, and food staff spend U.S.D
4.00 daily per one person on board.
    (signed: Master Henry L. S. Eng)

The report of the Coast Guard, of which I also have a copy,
is much more complicated, due to the Coast Guard lingo
and abbreviations. This is a summary:

    The following stations were involved in the
    rescue operation: Saba Radio Station; Virgin
    Gorda Police Station; Antilles Rescue
    Foundation;
    Roosevelt Roads Naval Air Station;
    Borinquen (Puerto Rico) Air Station
    and the refueling station on St. Maarten.
    One rescue vessel dispatched from Saba.
    Aircraft dispatched from Air Station
    Borinquen : HU25, HH3F, CGNR 2140 and
    CGNR 1494. Four sorties flown, a total of
    11.8 hours, 0.9 hrs in search.

The coordinates of the *PACIFIC FREEDOM* statement and the Coast Guard report coincided on 17-34 N, 63-48 W. The weather and sea conditions on Captain Eng's report were "fresh breeze, sea 5-7 feets." The Coast Guard reported "wind East at 15 kn, seas at 4 ft."

We received royal treatment on board the *PACIFIC FREEDOM*. The steward assigned Ken to the guest suite, Jeff to the owner's suite, and he put me up in the less luxurious pilot's stateroom. Each had a private bath.

"I am going to cry a little now," said Ken and gave both Jeff and me a hug. He did that often. Ken was a warm and loving man.

Some of the crew donated items of clothing for us. At breakfast in the morning in the officer's mess, Ken wore a T-shirt with a Chinese dragon on it, pants that ended at mid-calf, and sandals about five sizes too small. Jeff looked almost normal in overalls and flip-flops. I had on a gym suit and wore my yellow rubber boots.

From the young second officer we learned that the rescue boat from Saba had been only twenty minutes away.

Captain Eng had refused the helicopter pilot's request to wait for the boat to take us, the survivors, off.

"We have appointment Cumaná, Venezuela. Cannot miss appointment. Too high cost," he explained to us. "Copter pilot say okay."

The 560 foot long *PACIFIC FREEDOM* was underway from Montreal to Venezuela with 26,000 tons of wheat.

*So, we are on the way to Venezuela. What an adventure!* "When will we arrive in Cumaná?" I asked.

"Tomorrow, Saturday, twelve noon. We one hour late. Must catch up. Very important."

Then he told us that he was on the bridge the night before. "I see S O S, very slowly. Look again, Ess-Ohh-Ess, very slowly. I say, better call captain."

"What happened then?"

"Captain give orders. First mate swing out lifeboat and rig pilot ladder. Men on stand-by. Then you come on board." He laughed. "First time rescue, captain and me. Captain and me good friends. Navigation school together."

The crew of the *PACIFIC FREEDOM*, Liberian registry, consisted of twenty-eight Taiwanese seamen. The food was authentic Chinese and not very good. Greasy noodles, dumplings in cabbage soup, shredded pork—I hope it was pork—and crisp, deep fried vegetables. Breakfast was some kind of pancakes. Green tea and an orange accompanied every meal. Cockroaches were ever present on the floor, on the tables and in every corner.

Ken had not overcome his seasickness. Even the slight movement of this big ship had an effect on him. He spent much time in his stateroom, sick.

"My sailing days are over," he told me. "I thought the trimaran would take care of my problem. Now I am sick here, too. I give up."

I asked him, "Was the boat's name HAPPY TIME when you bought it?"

"No. This was my fifth boat. I had dinghies when I lived in Chicago. Called them all Happy Time. Later, there were some happy times too when I sailed with my daughters on Long Island Sound in my *Catalina 24*, but I always got seasick. I thought, maybe a trimaran…" He trailed off, shook his head. "It's no use."

I wanted to know about the Snoopy on the surfboard, but did not ask. He was visibly shaken.

On Saturday, May 11, we passed Margarita Island, and exactly at twelve noon the *PACIFIC FREEDOM* docked at Cumaná.

When I lived in Ecuador, in the 1950s, I worked for some years with the agency for the German steamship line HAPAG. It was my job to go on board every German vessel that came into port. I knew the procedure of clearing a ship's entry and departure, and I was familiar with examining Bills of Lading and cargo manifests. I also used to prepare passenger declarations for Customs and Immigration.

Thirty years later, and in another Latin American country, the procedure was still the same. The vessel's agent arrived on board. With him came the health inspector, the Customs and Immigration officials. Guards and checkers took their positions at strategic posts. Truck drivers stopped their vehicles at the gate to the pier and received their orders. Vendors swarmed on board and conducted a lively commerce with the crew. Whisky, cigarettes, perfumes, watches, toys, cameras and clothing changed hands.

The serious official business between the port and the vessel unfolded in the offer's mess. It is customary that the officials coming on board be treated as guests. Whisky flowed freely; cigarettes, snacks and sandwiches were on the table. Papers, lists and documents passed back and forth between the parties.

Ken, Jeff and I, the three shipwreck survivors, became the center of attention for the man from Immigration. The vessel's agent praised Captain Eng for his diligence saving the lives of three helpless individuals who would have perished but for his selfless assistance.

This did not impress the Immigration inspector. Slowly getting drunk, he demanded documentation that did not exist. Jeff's and my passports lay on the table, but Ken had no papers with which to identify himself.

Voices increased in volume with the amount of liquor consumed. The little Immigration guy got belligerent. The Venezuelans did not speak English, the Chinese did not speak Spanish.

Captain Eng sat back and left the negotiations to his second officer, his friend, who spoke the best English among the Chinese.

To put an end to the three-way language barrier, I revealed that I spoke fluent Spanish. Tensions relaxed. I interpreted and we got back to the business at hand. The agent drew up papers that allowed Ken to disembark. The drunk Immigration official signed them.

Meanwhile the discharging of the cargo had begun. Trucks pulled up on the pier alongside the vessel, an oversized vacuum cleaner hose sucked the wheat out of the belly of the ship and spewed it into the trucks.

I asked the overseeing clerk, " How do you account for the cargo?"

"By the rise of the vessel in the water, as it get's lighter."

This answer puzzled me. "How accurate can that be?"

"Not very," he said, "but it is not important. Half the cargo is destined for Cumaná; the rest goes to La Guaira. The trucks pass the weigh station when they come in empty, and then loaded when the leave. The difference is the net weight."

That made more sense to me. I guessed, a couple of tons more in one port and less in the other didn't matter—at least not to us. Our main concern was to obtain some decent clothing and the most urgent necessities.

We ventured into town. I felt an inexplicable lightness, free from all burden and responsibility. I did not have one single thing, object or matter to take care of. I had nothing but my own self, a passport that stated who I was and a credit card in my wallet.

This carefree existence was a new experience for me, and I liked it. Still in my yellow sea boots, my step was springy, and no preoccupation hampered my unencumbered mind.

Ken recovered from his seasickness quickly after the *PACIFIC FREEDOM* had docked in Cumaná. We walked down the pier into the neat streets of this small port and soon realized what a curious sight we were to the town's people. Three gringos in strange attire, one tall and lanky, one with long blond hair and one little guy in yellow boots.

Our first stop was a nickel-and-dime type store. Three toothbrushes, three combs, three T-shirts, three sets of underwear and three pairs of socks. Jeff and I bought sneakers; they didn't have Ken's size. For him we bought the largest sandals we could find. With the pants he had more trouble. The longest jeans available ended halfway up his calves. We easily found my sizes. Jeff was content with his overalls. We charged all our purchases to my credit card; I was the only one with the means to pay.

Back on board, Captain Eng assured us that the ship would be our home for as long as we needed it, or as long as it remained in port. The alternative would have been for us to go to a hotel. We were grateful for his courtesy and invited him to a drink in town.

He declined. "Thank you, but busy with insurance man. Cargo forward hold little wet from storm in St. Lawrence River."

It was Saturday, and the travel agency was closed for the afternoon. All further steps had to be postponed until Monday.

We, the three shipwrecked sailors, donned our new clothes and went to the *Hotel Marina* to celebrate our deliverance with a bottle of wine in the hotel bar.

Sunday, May 12, was Mother's Day. Cumaná was in a festive mode. In the morning we saw people in their Sunday fineries crowding into the churches, boys uncomfortable in their suits and neckties, girls dressed in white, with hats and ribbons, carrying flowers. In the afternoon, the streets and plazas and parks were deserted.

I think the three of us shared the happy-go-lucky, devil-may-care euphoria. We rented a car and drove along the rugged North coast of Venezuela as far as Puerto La Cruz. Here, too, the streets were empty. The people took Mother's Day seriously and celebrated *el Dia de la Madre* in their homes.

In Puerto La Cruz I overcame my reluctance to inform family and friends in New York of my whereabouts and the circumstances that brought me here. It was easy to make a collect call from a phone booth.

Carlos was the first to hear the news. "Are you all right? Unhurt? How are you, I mean emotionally?"

"I am fine, wonderful! Never been better! The three of us have unloaded all our excessive belongings and worries. We lost everything, and it feels great."

"I don't understand…"

I interrupted him. "Okay, I guess you have to experience it. Tell Mom and Susi that I am fine. Gotta go now. I guess we'll be flying home in a couple of days."

Then I called The Cat. "Hi The Cat, guess where I am."

"You tell me. Back in the States? Can't be on the ocean. So tell me already."

"I'm on the phone." (My standard answer whenever she asked where I was.) "You won't believe this: I am in Venezuela. We shipwrecked and a huge freighter picked us up."

"You what? Shipwrecked? You could have drowned. Venezuela, huh? Little Venezia, Italy, you know."

"Yeah, I know, but this one is in South America."

"Okay, I got that. So, tell me all about it when you get back. Ciao." She never liked long phone talks.

I had complied with my obligations and felt even better than before. We drove back to our home, the *PACIFIC FREEDOM.*

The vessel's agent, Victor Nuñez, was on board, waiting for us. He engaged Captain Eng in conversation, neither one of them speaking the other's language. Nuñez tried to be funny, laughing loudly, insensitively putting himself on the same level with the captain who was visibly annoyed.

Nuñez saw us coming up the gangway and he called us over. He addressed me in Spanish. "I came to take you out on the town, some fun place. You know, have some fun, some drinks and… there are girl, too. Come on, let's go."

We were not in the mood for the kind of fun this man had in mind. On the other hand, it wasn't easy to find an excuse. When Captain Eng reluctantly nodded his okay, we agreed as well.

Nuñez had come by jeep and brought another man with him. "Let's take your car. We can't all fit in the jeep."

I drove, and Nuñez directed me. "Straight this way, out of town, three or four miles. Mas rápido! Can't you go any faster?" *What an annoying man.*

We arrived at a solitary house with a red lantern in front. "Pull up here," said Nuñez.

Ken and Jeff, the captain and I looked at each other in puzzlement. What did Victor Nuñez have in mind? He and his friend were happily looking forward to a great evening.

Hesitatingly we stepped out of the car and into the saloon. This being Mother's Day, the proprietress evidently did not expect customers and quickly set up tables and chairs, asked what we would like to drink, and then called upstairs for some girls to come down.

A bottle of scotch, an ice bucket, bottled water and glasses on the table, we sat down, feeling very uncomfortable. Our embarrassment grew even more when the girls came down and Nuñez asked with no sense of propriety, "Qual te gusta? Which one do you like?"

This Red Light establishment must have been on the lowest end on the scale of whorehouses. The girls were unappetizing, ranging in age from sixteen to forty, and maybe the youngest was younger, the oldest older.

"Ninguna?" asked Nuñez. "You don't like any of them?"

Now everybody was embarrassed, including the females.

Captain Eng, most displeased, gestured that he would like to leave. We left half a bottle of scotch on the table. Victor Nuñez and his friend showed their disappointment and so did the women. The captain and the three of us were relieved.

Nuñez, however, did not give up yet. He gave directions to another, "better place," but I ignored him and found my way back to the ship. Captain Eng, shy and embarrassed, deeply humiliated, said good night and went to his quarters.

"What an evening," said Ken and shook his head. "What the hell did this Victor what's-his-name think, taking us to a place like that?"

"Those women…" Jeff was not amused. "Did you see the one without teeth? What did they take us for?"

"A pair of idiots, this Victor and his friend," I said. "Glad, that's over."

We went each to our assigned staterooms.

The local papers, of which I have a copy, had printed our story. The headline, in super large letters, read: RESCATADOS CON VIDA TRES NAUFRAGOS! (Three shipwreck survivors rescued.) The story was told with many errors and gross exaggerations. Here is part of it in translation:

*The shipwrecked persons had left Virgin*
*Gorda in the yacht Happy Time and*
*foundered the second day at sea. They were*
*rescued by the freighter Pacific Freedom, of*
*Liberian flag, under the command of*
*Captain Eng Li Sam. They were identified*
*as: Belfrin Kenneth, 63 years old,*
*Psychologist; Larren Jeffrey, 18, student,*
*both North Americans; and Hasse Peter, 57*
*businessman, of German nationality.*
The report continues:
*While in the custody of the Director of*
*Immigration, they were subjected to*
*intense medical examinations.*

It is my guess that the drunken *Director de Inmigración* had his hand in the concoction of the newspaper article, especially of that last false statement.

Our first matter of business on Monday morning was get new glasses for Ken. He had saved neither his contact lenses nor his glasses.

We found an *Oculista.* Ken had to read the chart. I translated for the doctor, mistakes included, so that he could prescribe the correct eyeglasses. This little interlude caused great amusement for Jeff and me.

On our way from the eye doctor to the travel agency, a gentleman stopped us on the street. Three conspicuous gringos could not hide in this small town.

"Manuel Alvarez," he introduced himself. "If ever you should need any assistance, do not hesitate to call on me." He handed each of us his business card. *INGETECA, Ingenieros & Tecnicos Asociados. Manuel Alvarez, Administrador.*

We thanked him; he obviously had noble intentions.

This card was the first object of any value in our hands. We had to keep it safe, but it was a burden to us.

"I don't want this card," said Jeff. "You want it?"

Ken and I looked at each other. Did we want the card? No, we were happier without it. Stuff to take care of... It would mean the end of our carefree days.

*What a weird feeling, not wanting any possessions. Like the return of memory after a spell of amnesia. Like waking up from a coma, having to face reality.*

The young woman at the travel agency was extraordinarily beautiful. Her evenly dark complexion, green eyes and short black hair were in delicate harmony with the rose colored blouse she wore with a pale beige pantsuit.

She booked the three of us on an afternoon flight to Maiquetia. From there, Jeff wanted to hitchhike to Caracas and stay a few more days in Venezuela. Obviously, he would arrange to get some money from his parents. Ken booked a flight to Miami, and I decided to fly back to New York and immediately look for another boat in need of crew.

Jeff accompanied Ken to pick up his new, steel-rimmed glasses. I asked the attractive travel agent to have lunch with me, but she declined. She could not leave the office unattended. When I insisted a little more strongly, she said she would have lunch later, with her husband. I considered my appearance: a cheap T-shirt with *Cumaná* written on it, ill-fitting jeans and blue sneakers, bought at a nickel-and-dime store. How could this gorgeous, exquisitely dressed woman have accepted my invitation?

Ken, Jeff and I met for lunch at a little outdoors café. Jeff had found the *Oficina de Teléfonos* and sent a telegram to his parents, asking for money.

For the last time we went back to the ship. We found Captain Eng in his office and thanked him for his hospitality. The first and second mates and the radio operator sat in the officer's mess. We shook hands with all of them.

The second officer said, "Why you leaving? We go La Guaira tomorrow. You find flight home there."

"We already made our arrangements," said Ken and we thanked them again. I found a plastic garbage bag and retrieved my foul weather jacket, life vest and rubber boots from my cabin. I stuffed all of it into the plastic bag, together with the T-shirt and gym shorts I wore at the time of our rescue.

I met Ken at the gangway. He had his life jacket, his only possession, over his arm. Jeff, still in his overalls, joined us. On deck were several of the Chinese Crewmen we had become friends with. We had a lively good-bye, calling back and forth, waving farewell as we walked down to the pier.

The rental car stood near the gangway. We felt nostalgic leaving the *PACIFIC FREEDOM*. Less than five days we had spent on the ship, yet it felt like home to us. As we drove away, more shouts of good-bye and good luck, more waving, more laughter accompanied us until I turned the car from the pier into the town of Cumaná and toward the road to the airport.

"That was a beautiful lady at the travel agency, Pete. I have never seen such eyes," said Ken as we drove to the airport.

"I asked her to have lunch with me," I said. "She didn't accept, but she was very nice about it. You saw how she was dressed? And look at me!" I laughed. "Besides, she is married."

"I thought you might ask her out. I saw how you looked at her."

Jeff said, "There will be plenty of good-looking girls in Caracas. That lady must have been at least thirty."

I turned the car in at the shack with the *Por Alquiler* sign. We were right on time for the three-fifty departure and boarded the little twin-engined plane for the half hour-flight to Maiquetia.

A taxi drove us to *Las Quince Letras*, in the town of Macuto. This small hotel, situated on a cliff directly above the beach, had a restaurant attached to it. Sitting at a table on the ample terrace, we ordered a gigantic meal of fish and seafood: shrimp and lobster, baked *merluza* and seared tuna, with yellow rice, salad and garlic bread. Combined with a splendid view over the wide-open ocean, it was a memorable farewell dinner.

The hotel management provided a cot in addition to the two beds in the room we had rented. I, the smallest among us, volunteered to sleep on the cot. The heavy meal and the espresso I had afterwards kept me awake much of the night.

Ken also complained of restless sleep, preoccupied with the loss of his *HAPPY TIME V* and in contemplation of his future. Jeff, at the age of eighteen, did not bother with such worries and slept soundly through the night.

Ken and I had to leave the hotel early in the morning for our flight to Miami. Jeff came with us and we said good-bye in the American Airlines lounge at Simon Bolívar International Airport.

Ken, with tears in his eyes, embraced Jeff. "Good luck, my boy. Have your adventure, but don't forget us. We must have a reunion in a month or two in New York."

Jeff promised to keep in touch. We shook hands and slapped each other on the shoulders. Then he walked away toward the exit to find a ride to Caracas.

Ken and I boarded the plane for Miami, on schedule for departure at eight-fifteen. He folded his long legs into the inadequate space between the seats.

"Pete," he said as the airplane taxied for lift-off, forgive me if I am quiet. I want to be alone with my thoughts."

There was not much to say. What we had experienced together needed no words. "I know, Ken. We lived through something that will bind us together for life. We will definitely have a reunion in New York."

We had a heartfelt parting in Miami. Ken stood and watched me as I walked away to the gate for my flight to New York.

Peter Haase

# MACHETE

The taxi driver looked at me as if to say, "Can this guy pay the fare?"

As I stood outside the arrivals building at La Guardia hailing a cab, I could have been mistaken for a bum from lower Manhattan. Four days in the same T-shirt and cheap jeans, sneakers and in my hand a rumpled garbage bag with a life vest sticking out of it—the picture of a bearded, homeless man of the Bowery.

I arrived at Julia's house in Queens, only a few blocks from the airport. When she opened the door, she had the same incredulous look on her face as the taxi driver. Then she burst out laughing. "You look as if they just fished you out of the East River!"

"I know, I can't show my face anywhere. Can I perhaps borrow a shirt from Carlos? His pants won't fit me." Carlos was almost six feet tall.

"Why don't you go to your girlfriend? That's where all your clothes are, isn't it?" She was still laughing, but there was a little sting in her tone.

"I am sorry, yes. But I came in at La Guardia, practically next door, and my car is here."

Carlos came up from the basement. "Hi Dad. You just got here? You look a little shabby, but otherwise all right."

I gave him a hug and asked, "Is Susi coming?" She lived with her aunt in Manhattan. "Then I don't have to tell my story twice."

"I'll give her a call. Are you staying here?"

"Actually, Carlos, I wanted to ask you if you needed the car. I want to go and get myself some decent clothes. I just asked Mom if I could borrow one of your shirts."

"You are welcome to stay overnight, if that suits you," said Julia.

Susi came in the evening. It was a complete family reunion. Telling my story, I relived the last six weeks, which seemed to me more like six months. So much had happened in such a short time. The hardest part for me was to explain why I joined Ken Helprin knowing that his boat was less than seaworthy.

"I like Ken. He is a genuinely nice man. I knew it was a bad decision, but I couldn't say no. Besides, I was the only one on board with any common sense in seamanship, and who knew how to signal SOS. Maybe, I saved their lives. Who knows?"

Julia put me up in the small bedroom that Carlos had occupied before he moved into the basement.

The following morning I drove to Brooklyn. It was Wednesday and The Cat had taken the day off.

"Hi, I was just going out. You come with me? I want to get discount tickets for CATS on Broadway."

"Don't you want to hear what happened?"

"Yeah, I know. You shipwrecked. How was your flight from Venezuela?"

I gave her a long hug. She felt so good in my arms, my story didn't matter anymore and she forgot about the tickets for *CATS*.

A week after my return to New York, I drove to Newport, Rhode Island to find a boat in need of crew. I talked to some people on the docks, in the bars and at the Seaman's Church Institute. Besides receiving some hints and suggestions, I was not successful in my search.

Before driving back to New York, I pinned prepared notices on bulletin boards and a sailor's bookstore, at a ship chandlers and at the main yacht pier.

> *Experienced crew available.*
> *Sail anytime – Anywhere.*
> *Please call daytime: (The Cat's office*
> *Number) Or evenings (her home*
> *phone)*

When I came back from Newport late that night, The Cat was already in bed. She handed me a note.

"This man called half an hour ago. Spoke funny English. I didn't get his name right. Hopple, Noddle, Noodle—something like that. First name Francisco, I think."

"Oh, thanks. I hope you got the number right."

The Cat was a receptionist; she should be able to take a message.

"You are a good receptionist, aren't you?"

"The best. You know that."

In the morning I called the number The Cat had scribbled down. Francisco Hobel answered, and indeed, he had a strange accent.

"Are you German?" was the first thing he asked.

"Yes," I answered. I am from Germany. Where are you from?"

"Well, ich bin originally from Hungary." He spoke German to me, mixed with English. Yo vivo en Venezuela." He now added Spanish to the mix and continued to intermingle the three languages.

I answered in Spanish. "How long have you lived in Venezuela?"

"Almost twenty years. Ich bin citizen de Venezuela," he said in the tri-lingual language of his own.

"So, I guess you have a boat and want to sail to Venezuela. I just came from there. I can drive up to Newport anytime to meet you," I said in English.

"My boat needs some finishing touches. It is ganz neu, launched just last month. The interior is unfinished. In a couple of weeks it should be ready."

"Sounds good to me. When should I come and meet you, see the boat and discuss the details?"

"I would like you to come pronto, to help with preparations. Mucho trabajo before departure. Can you come mañana?"

*Oh boy, this guy is in a hurry. We haven't even met yet.* "Give me a few days. Next Monday all right with you?"

"Sure. The boat is at anchor, far out in the harbor. Ask water taxi man to take you out to the *MACHETE.*"

*Another home-built boat? I just shipwrecked on one!*

"Okay, I'll see you on board then on Monday, around noon."

*Machete, huh? I wonder what this is going to be like. And again Venezuela? What a coincidence.*

On the weekend, The Cat went to Long Island to visit her mother. I had the opportunity to do a lot of shopping, which I do much better alone.

82

At Goldberg's Marine in mid-town Manhattan, I bought a lightweight foul weather suit and two pairs of topsiders. Then I drove to the mall in Paramus, New Jersey, to buy shorts, shirts and underwear, a sweat suit, T-shirts, socks and a crewneck sweater. I knew this was only a minimum of what I needed, but it had to do. It was not possible to replace everything I had lost when the *HAPPY TIME V* went down.

In a luggage store, I found a canvas duffel bag and a knapsack. I still needed a sleeping bag.

Early on Monday morning, I packed my new treasures into the Honda and drove again to Newport. I left my bags in the car and walked to the dock. The water taxi driver knew where the *MACHETE* was anchored.

"That boat? Have you seen it yet?"

"No. What's the matter with it?" His tone, this question, made me curious.

"You'll see. Not that there is anything wrong with it. It's just weird. Looks like... Well, you can see for yourself."

He zigzagged through the crowded anchorage. Way out there, we approached a long, flat hull of bright mahogany, beautifully varnished, with three black masts and sails covered in white canvas.

"That's the MACHETE," he said and pulled up at the stern to a kind of landing platform. "Here we are. That's two bucks. Are you going to crew in her?"

"I don't know yet," I answered and paid him. Then I called out, "Permission to come on board."

Francisco Hobel, in his late forties, was a smaller, younger version of Kenneth Helprin. His formerly reddish hair and beard had thinned and grayed considerably. His appearance, demeanor and speech struck me immediately as unconventional, even eccentric.

The *MACHETE* reflected this quality in her design. The boat was as unusual as her owner. Sixty feet in length she had a beam of only fourteen feet. Her deck was as flat as that of an aircraft carrier.

Francisco was friendly and he gladly answered my questions. I learned that he had studied engineering in Germany. Modestly, but not entirely without pride, he named some official and public buildings in Caracas, which he had designed.

He told me in his mish-mash of languages, "I drew up the plan for the MACHETE with the help of ingeniero naval. The idea was to build a fast boat. We borrowed the best Qualitäten for that purpose from different design concepts con el resultado this innovative prototipo exótico."

From a large envelope he extracted some photographs showing the boat in various stages of construction. Pointing to the last one, he said excitedly, "This was taken on her maiden voyage. The MACHETE under full sail."

I saw a cross between a converted speedboat and a Chinese Junk. Three black masts carried brown sails of an unusual full shape. The only elevation from the flat deck was the cockpit at the stern of the vessel.

Francisco and I stood in the cockpit; he called it the steering station. Under the wide windshield was a dashboard, which eventually would house the instruments and controls. The side windows had been swung up and fastened under the ceiling. There were no seats. The five-foot long tiller was a beautiful curved piece of art, made of laminated oriental wood. It took up half the length of the steering station.

"I find it surprising that a vessel of this size has a tiller instead of a wheel," I said.

"We wanted to preserve an element of antiquity and originality. Don't you think a wheel would disturb the basic design? It would upset my sense of harmony."

*He is eccentric, all right.* I complimented him, "You are an artist, as well as an engineer and an architect."

Francisco invited me to come below and I followed him down the companionway. In the stern, there was a comfortable cabin with adjacent bathroom. "Captains quarter," he explained.

The rest of the hull in its entire length below decks was unfinished. There was the outline of a huge tub. "This will be the Jacuzzi. For now we cover it and we can use it as crew quarters." He turned around and showed me several brand new mattresses stacked against a partition.

"Where is the engine?" I asked.

"There is no engine."

"Wow, no engine. A real sailboat." *If only it were more conventional, not so extreme, so outlandish.*

Francisco led the way up on deck. We walked to the main mast, which was so thick, no man could get his arms around it.

"Teardrop shape for wind efficiency," he explained. "All three masts are freestanding. No shrouds, no stays. They rotate on ball bearings as the booms swing out."

The foremast stood in the very bow of the boat. There was no jib. The smallest of the masts, the mizzen, was aft of the steering station on the landing platform, or swim platform.

"In addition to the three sails we can use staysails, rigged between the masts. She should be capable of twelve to fifteen knots, in the right conditions. Did you have lunch? I am just about ready here. Vamos a mi casa."

We got into his Boston Whaler, which had a powerful outboard motor on its transom. I was impressed by the unconventionality of both the *MACHETE* and her owner-designer. Throughout the conversation, Francisco mixed English, German and Spanish. I already began to respond in the same way.

Following his directions, I drove with him to the house where he lived with his fiancée, Anita. On the way I gave him a quick run-down of my experiences, including the shipwreck of the *HAPPY TIME V*.

"Don't tell Anita anything about hat. She would be terrified. She is scared enough as it is." He saw my skeptical look. "No, no. She's not sailing with us, va a Caracas en avion."

Anita was an attractive blond woman, much younger than Francisco.

"You can stay here, or live on the boat," she said after I had been introduced to her. "It's your choice."

I noticed her New England accent. "Thank you, but I haven't talked with Francisco yet about anything concerning my participation in the voyage."

We ate crackers and chips with salsa, smoked fish and cheese dip. Anita served white wine.

I turned to Francisco. "When do you plan to leave? What are the conditions?"

"We can make the arreglos right now. I want to leave in three weeks, July the first at the latest. I'll pay you one thousand dollars and the plane ticket back home."

This I had not expected. I almost choked on my cracker and swallowed some wine. "Fine with me." For a second I was too surprised to say anything else, but then I caught myself. "I have most of my stuff in the car. I can sleep on the boat tonight, if that's all right with you. I just need to buy a sleeping bag."

"There are blankets on board. You can get your sleeping bag later."

"I have to go back to New York for a week or so. Some matters to take care of. After that, I am ready to stay on board for whatever needs to be done."

86

"We will need one more person. A young man came around the other day. I don't know if he will show up. A German guy. Seemed all right to me."

I said good night to Francisco and Anita, and drove back to the harbor. I had become a paid delivery crewman. Before taking the water taxi out to the *MACHETE*, I went into a bar, had a bowl of chowder and a beer. Then I took my bags out of the car and signaled the taxi.

On the dock stood a young fellow, as if he were waiting for me. "Are you going out to the MACHETE?" he asked me.

*That must be the German guy Francisco mentioned to me.* I said, "Yes, why?"

"I am his crew member. My name is Ulf. Didn't he tell you? What's your name?"

"No he didn't tell me. He mentioned someone who didn't show up, so he lost interest."

I found his attitude impertinent and did not give him my name.

"Well, can I come with you?" His curly blond hair was waving in the wind.

"No, you certainly can not. I can't bring strangers on board. That should be clear to you."

"I need a place to sleep. I am broke. I swear, I have talked to Francisco."

"Sorry. Go to the Seaman's Institute. They'll put you up."

With that I boarded the taxi and left Ulf standing on the dock.

"I've seen that guy hanging out here," said the taxi man. "I once took him out to the MACHETE. The owner paid his fair. The guy is a bum, hasn't got a penny to his name."

"I am sorry, but I can't just take him on board without the owner's permission."

"Sure can't."

Early the next morning Francisco came in the dinghy, the Boston Whaler, and he brought Ulf with him.

"Ulf will be joining us after all," said Francisco.

That's not good, I thought. Ulf took on an arrogant posture, as if to say: see, told you so.

Francisco did not seem to notice. He was either naïve or a pushover. Ulf had finagled himself into Francisco's confidence and I had to make sure to assert my status on board as first mate.

I remained in Newport for a few days, helping Francisco with procuring materials and accessories. He bought rope and chain, bales of fiberglass, rolls of canvas and carpet, gallons of paint and buckets of resin. I made dozens of trips with the Boston Whaler between the *MACHETE* and the dock.

Ulf turned out to be a lazy bum. Every time I arrived at the boat, I had to call him, wait until he appeared and then he was slow and clumsy in handling the stuff I brought. He was careless and uncooperative. In the middle of a job he asked me for a cigarette and took a break. Once, in a downpour, he had the nerve to put on my foul weather jacket, leaving me in my shirtsleeves.

I did not tell Francisco about the situation with Ulf; I thought it would be better he found out by himself. For some reason, I don't know why, Francisco seemed to like him.

The weather had been cold, rainy and miserable the entire time I spent in Newport and it was raining the day I drove back to New York. Our shipwreck reunion was planned for the weekend. Ken, who was staying with his friend Golden in New Jersey, had made reservations for Saturday, June 9 at O'Henry's in the Village.

Jeff Darren came on his Guzzi motorcycle from Vermont. Over lunch we rehashed from all angles the incident we had experienced together. Everyone remembered a moment or a detail the others had forgotten or had not been aware of.

Jeff asked, "at what time did you cut the dinghy loose?"

"I never did," I answered. "It must have followed the boat down to the bottom." I turned to Ken. "Did you see what was left of the HAPPY TIME from the deck of the freighter?"

"I didn't look down. I was in pretty bad shape." He shook his head. "I don't know how I made it up the Jacob's ladder."

"I saw nothing when I looked over the rail, although it was as bright as daylight. Jeff, since when was that helicopter there?"

"We were still standing on the cabin roof, just before we started to climb. Without that light, I don't think we would have found the ladder. But the HAPPY TIME? I didn't see her either. Must have sunk the moment we were off."

And so it went. We spoke fondly of Captain Eng and the friendly crew of the *PACIFIC FREEDOM*. We laughed remembering the drunken Immigration man and that awful evening with Victor Nuñez.

"Here, I still have the card Manuel Alvarez gave me." Ken held up the card. "And I am sure you didn't forget the pretty travel agent." He smiled and nudged me lightly with his foot under the table.

Jeff talked little about his side trip to Caracas. Perhaps he did not have such a good time. But he told us he had decided to go to college after all. "I'll start in the fall," he said and we applauded him.

We all had lost what we carried with us that day in the Anegada passage, but Jeff and I were aware that Ken had lost the most: his precious boat—decrepit, but precious to him.

He looked sad. "It was my last attempt at sailing, my last boat." Then he became more animated. "I will go around the world, though, but it won't be in a boat. I booked a Round-the-Globe tour with British Overseas Airways. Three months, beginning in May next year."

"Congratulations, Ken! That's great!" Jeff and I said together, and then I told them I already found another boat. "Back to Venezuela. I'm leaving in a couple of weeks."

"You just won't quit, huh, Pete? I wish you the best of luck." Ken reached across the table to shake my hand.

It was a three-hour luncheon. Jeff had the long trip back to Vermont ahead of him. I drove Ken to the Port Authority Bus Terminal and then went back to Brooklyn. The Cat was not going out to Long Island that weekend and I was looking forward to spending Sunday with her. I stayed for a whole week.

We haven't had such a good time together since our break-up. It seemed we were getting along best in a temporary relationship, of short duration. By the end of the week, it was time to move on.

"The Cat, I discovered this in the pocket of my foul weather jacket," I said to her as we said good-bye. "I bought it for you in Martinique." The coral bracelet; I had forgotten all about it. "Look, it survived the ordeal in the Anegada Passage with me, and I didn't know I had it in my breast pocket all the time."

"Yeah, thanks. Does that mean it's extra special? I put it with the rest of the stuff you gave me over the years."

The Cat—she's just not a sentimentalist, and I love her for that, too.

On Sunday, June 17 I returned to Newport. Susi came with me to drive the car back to New York. She wanted to see the weird boat I had tried to describe to her.

90

We went out to the *MACHETE* and she met Francisco and Ulf. The weather remained blustery and rainy. Newport harbor was gray and dismal.

After lunch in a smoky tavern, I sent Susi on her way. "Drive carefully in the rain, Susi. I'll give you a call this evening to see that you made it all right. Then I can have peace of mind."

"I'll be all right, Dad. Take care of yourself. Don't sink! Wear your harness."

We still had a week before our departure. Preparations continued. Francisco loaded all of his personal belongings on board. The interior of the *MACHETE* soon looked like a moving van.

In the evenings we were often at the house with Francisco and Anita.

Francisco talked about his plans. "I have the design for the staterooms, the saloon and the Jacuzzi all ready in blueprint. Carpenters and joiners will need weeks, perhaps months, to finish the interior. It will be muy elegante." He was enthusiastic. "When it is finally ready, I intend to cruise con mi familia y amigos for a few months, and then hire the boat out for charter tours in the southern Caribbean. Aruba, Bonaire, Curaçao and Panamá." He added, "Luxury cruises."

Anita spoke only English, with a few phrases in Spanish here and there. Ulf, who spoke passable English, usually sat quietly at the table, ate their food, drank their wine and smoked their cigarettes. I don't know how much he understood of the conversations. Francisco spoke in his mishmash of languages, especially when he got enthusiastic.

Ulf and I slept on board. He was brazen enough to install himself in the captain's quarters. I set up a mattress on top of the unfinished Jacuzzi. For the time being I was comfortable there, but it would not be a good place once we were at sea.

91

The end of June came and still the weather was raw and unfriendly. Low, gray clouds were hanging over the harbor of Newport. Rain, drizzle and gusty winds made life miserable.

At last, June 30 we declared our departure at Customs. Ulf and I had German passports. Francisco was a citizen of Venezuela, and the *MACHETE* sailed under the Venezuelan flag. The first day of July, a Sunday, was stormy and we postponed our departure for one more day. On Monday the sky began to clear. At four-thirty in the afternoon we hoisted the foresail and the mizzen, dropped the mooring cable and headed toward open water. At long last at sea again.

Francisco entrusted Ulf with the Boston Whaler to push and nudge the big boat out of the harbor. The wind was too light to maneuver the *MACHETE* through the anchorage. Soon, however, we encountered a fresh breeze of twelve to fifteen knots from the southwest, and with it came the fog.

While I was at the tiller, Francisco and Ulf hoisted first the outboard motor on board, and then the dinghy. I put the tiller on automatic pilot and helped them winch the huge sail up the main mast.

The *MACHETE* picked up speed and before night fell we left Block Island to starboard and Nantucket to port. We saw neither of those two islands because we were completely fogged in. Once we were sure to have cleared Montauk on the eastern tip of Long Island, we steered 150 degrees, or about southeast, heading straight for Bermuda.

The night air was cool and damp. Everything was dripping wet from the fog. The first night at sea is always an exciting event and we did not feel a desire for sleep. The battery that powered the autohelm ran down and we resorted to manual steering. The two solar panels on the roof of the steering station had not received a ray of sunlight for over a week.

The only electronics on board the *MACHETE* were the autohelm, a radio direction finder and the two-way VHF radio. These three instruments depended on the storage battery, which depended on the solar panels, which depended on the generosity of the sun.

I liked to be at the tiller. Ulf was too careless and I did not trust him with anything that required some degree of dedication. So, the job of helmsman fell to me. Francisco most of the time was otherwise occupied, and Ulf shunned everything that was work or a job.

Our compass, the only one we had, was a small handheld device like those the boy scouts use on their excursions into the woods. Since we could not turn on the lights, for lack of electricity, I could not see the compass bearing and from time to time used a flashlight to verify the course.

The second day at sea brought us some improvement in the weather, but it was still cold when the sun hid behind the clouds. Francisco, who often stayed below, had set up a drawing board under the big skylight and worked on plans for a future project. By midday he called Ulf to help him with some fiberglass work to strengthen the center bulwark. I was more or less excluded from their activities. It seemed to be a nuisance for them when I called to be relieved at the helm.

There was hardly any change in wind or weather and no adjustments to the sails or our course were necessary. The average speed was a steady eight knots.

In the afternoon Ulf caught a fish. We did not know what kind it was, but it weighed at least six pounds. I filleted the fish and prepared a pretty good meal for supper, but I had no intention to become the cook on board, in addition to helmsman. Those are the two jobs on a boat nobody likes.

Before nightfall the air became warmer and balmier. We were entering the Gulf Stream. The sun had generated some charge in the battery and I put the helm on automatic, at least for short intervals.

Fourth of July. No fireworks, no celebration, just a warm breeze and hazy sunshine. We shed sweaters and rain gear, donned shorts and T-shirts. By dead reckoning, we were about 350 miles out of Newport and 500 off the coast of Maryland. We met one sailboat, heading north. Our radio was too weak to make contact.

Francisco and Ulf finally agreed on an arrangement for night watches. The first two nights I stood watch from one to five in the morning; now we were going to rotate so that everyone could enjoy some decent hours of sleep.

The radio direction finder picks up signals in the line of sight. As long as the transmitter is below the horizon, the instrument cannot receive the signal. We headed for Bermuda, but a few degrees off course, and we would never see it. Francisco and Ulf fiddled with the sextant; neither one of them knew more about celestial navigation than I, and they argued about a method to calculate our position. On the fifth day out of Newport, Francisco had us thirty miles north of Bermuda. That could not be right because so close we would be able to receive radio signals. Ulf's position was east of Bermuda, in the middle of the Atlantic.

The following day I asked Francisco, "Let me take a noon shot of the sun? I just want to see how close I come to your observation."

"Good idea. Let's all take an observation and compare. Then we figure out the average."

I had my own method, learned from a book entitled *Introduction to Celestial Navigation*. Perusing the Nautical Almanac and the conversion tables, I arrived at a position eighty miles north of Bermuda. Francisco was closer to the islands, Ulf farther out in the Atlantic. The average would have put us within radio distance, but we never got a signal, which meant we were all wrong.

For several days we had light wind. The weather turned hot and humid and we waited for the trade winds to set in from the east. If we were where we thought we were, we should head due south for the Anegada Passage and the Caribbean.

I usually took my showers on the swim platform, pouring buckets of seawater over me. Francisco suggested taking a swim in the relatively calm ocean surrounding us. One after the other, we attached our harnesses to a halyard and lowered ourselves over the port side into the sea. This was great fun, but a strenuous workout at the speed the boat made through the water.

In these lazy days, Ulf had strung a hammock in the cockpit. It took up the whole length between the windshield and the mizzenmast, dangling inches above the tiller. Francisco told me he did not like that, but he said nothing to Ulf. *Was he afraid of him?*

One week into the voyage we were still unsure of our position. Francisco ignored my opinion and relied on Ulf who seemed to intimidate him with his arrogant, insolent behavior.

Ulf was no sailor. I was sure of that, although he maintained he had been sailing for many years. I discovered that the only "sailing" he had done was on a freighter transporting locomotives from Bremen to somewhere in Africa; I believe he mentioned Mauritania. He was full of bullshit, but evidently he impressed Francisco.

"Don't you see what a fraud this arrogant bastard is," I asked Francisco. "He lies himself into your confidence and you believe every word he says. What about that hammock, huh? He inconveniences everyone on board and shows no concern." I pointed to the tiller. "Yesterday he sat on it; I heard it crack. Know what he did this morning? He asked me to bring him coffee, while he stayed in his hammock. The nerve this guy has! You put him in his place, or I will."

"Did you bring him his coffee?"

"You think I am his servant? Of course not. Maybe you would have."

Francisco had a little more respect for me after that discussion, but he did nothing about Ulf.

I took a sun sight at noon the following day and then figured out our position with Francisco. "31.00 degrees North Latitude, 57.30 degrees West Longitude. Southeast of Bermuda, you agree?"

"Time to head south. The trades will be with us today or tomorrow," he said excitedly, and to Ulf who was at the tiller, "New course, Ulf. One eighty. We're going south!"

We met a freighter, underway from New Orleans to Leningrad, and received our first accurate coordinates: 33.00 North, 54.00 West.

"Wow," I said, "we are much farther out in the Atlantic than we thought and just now passing Bermuda. I have to admit, Ulf was close the other day. So much more reason to head south."

We celebrated with two cups of whisky each.

The light wind continued for another day. Ulf caught a fish that looked like an eel. We cooked it, and there was just enough for a bite for each of us.

In the night the wind increased and we put a reef in the mainsail. I was on watch from one to five a m. Ulf came up to take over.

I said, "We must be making close to ten knots. Wind's southeast, twenty-five knots, course two-oh-five." I went below.

An hour later I awoke to a slam-bang crashing noise. The boat swung around, heeled sharply to the other side and kept turning. In an instant both Francisco and I were on deck.

"Was war das? Que pasó? What happened?" Francisco grabbed a towel; he was completely naked. "Did we just jibe?"

Jibing is turning the boat around so that the wind passes through the stern to the other side, a potentially dangerous maneuver when not under control.

Ulf came out of his hammock.

"He fell asleep. That could have taken the masts down." I turned to Francisco. "This man is careless and irresponsible. You see that now? If you don't order him to take that hammock down, I cut it down myself." I was outraged.

Ulf removed the hammock. In the morning I had another talk with Francisco.

"He is totally unreliable. You see that, don't you?"

"I know, but what can I do?" Francisco examined the tiller. "We can't jeopardize the harmony during the voyage." He saw the foot-long crack in the tiller. "I have to fix this with epoxy."

"What harmony? There is no harmony. Night watches from now on will be between you and me. We can't trust him. In a stronger wind we could have lost the masts," and pointing to the tiller, "You see the damage he has done already."

Later that day Ulf asked me for a cigarette. I had two left. In the name of harmony, I gave one to Ulf and we had our last smoke for the duration of the voyage.

We made radio contact with a freighter bound for Europe. Still sailing with a reef in the mainsail, we were happy with the progress we had made to the south and anticipated entering the Caribbean in seventy-two hours by way of the Anegada Passage.

On June 12, heavy clouds gathered. At four in the afternoon it was ominously calm, the sky dark gray.

Francisco was with me in the steering station. On our port bow, on the lightly undulating, leaden sea, we saw a cauldron of steaming water, twirling, coming toward us. A black funnel extended skyward.

As spray hit the windshield, the *MACHETE* heeled sharply to starboard, then came back violently and heeled to port.

Tossed about, we lost our footing. I clung to the tiller. Francisco slid backwards onto the swim platform and caught a line hanging from the mizzenmast. It saved him from being washed overboard.

Within seconds, the boat was back on an even keel. Ulf came up the companionway. "What happened?"

Still stunned and speechless, I pointed to the phenomenon just behind us. Ulf ran down and came back with his camera. By the time he was ready to take a picture, the funnel had dissipated, but I have in my album two photos showing the gray sea and the steaming cauldron, which we had sailed through.

Francisco was shaken but unhurt except for a bruise on his upper left arm. Ulf took over the helm.

The wind came around to the north and increased to forty-five knots. We headed into the wind that had turned cold, and Francisco took down the mainsail. We tried to sail before the wind, but Ulf could not bring the boat around. Under foresail and mizzen, we managed a westerly course, making great speed.

"Take down the mizzen!" Francisco yelled in the storm. "We are making too much speed."

I took the helm from Ulf, and he and Francisco hauled down the mizzen. With nothing but the foresail, I could not keep the boat on course and we were now running before the wind. The confused seas had built to eight to ten feet, the crests breaking and sending gushes of water over the bow. Rain mixed with saltwater hit the windscreen.

I closed the windows on port, the weather side.

At midnight, after eight hours at the helm, Francisco relieved me. I had called him to take over.

Exhausted, I slept solidly for six hours. When I awoke, the sea was perfectly calm.

Francisco examined the hull. There was some water in the bilge, which had been dry before the storm. Ulf and I set the mizzen and then I went below again. Francisco squeezed some putty along the keelson above the fin keel.

"It's a fifteen-foot keel," he said. "Like a racing sloop. It has worked itself loose in the twisting movements the boat made when we first were hit by the waterspout. Then in these violent seas. I tightened the bolts." With a special tool for this purpose, a two-foot long wrench, he had adjusted by a quarter turn every one of the eight bolts that hold the keel to the keelson. "I expected that some play might develop. It's a new boat."

We put three layers of fiberglass over the putty and when we checked later, the bilge was dry.

At noon another squall hit. The rain came down hard and visibility was less than fifty feet. I again was at the helm. My relations with Francisco were better since our talk and he trusted me at the tiller. He assigned other jobs to Ulf.

"The radar reflector has to come down," he said to him. "It slams against the mast constantly. It will break." In the lull that followed the squall he told him, "Put your harness on and take the damn thing down."

The reflector is a fiberglass drum, about two feet in length that is hoisted up the mast. The aluminum contents serve to make a boat more visible on the radar screen of a vessel within radar distance.

On the *MACHETE* we used the flag halyard to hoist the reflector to the top of the main mast. Ulf, more used to working on a freighter than on a yacht, manhandled the thin halyard as if it were a chain. The reflector came crashing down and broke in a hundred pieces as it hit the deck.

Francisco was upset, but Ulf got away with a mild, "Dammit, cant you be more careful?"

The storm intensified. On Sunday, July 14, we estimated the wind at fifty-five to sixty knots. Francisco insisted that we steer a course that would put the least amount of stress on hull and keel, regardless of our heading. The wind shifted constantly. At times I found myself steering north or northwest.

By keeping the seas on the starboard quarter, I eased the boat over the crests and only occasionally crashed into a rogue wave, which sent shudders through the hull.

Francisco, standing by my side much of the time, had a worried look on his face.

"Sorry," I said, and he saw I was doing my best. We judged some of the waves well over fifteen feet.

Sunday night and into Monday, there were thunderstorms north and west of us. The wind decreased to fifteen knots and turned south. By noon, before we saw some patches of blue in the sky, we hoisted the reefed main. Our course was now west, toward the Bahamas. The wind shifted more to the west and by evening we were sailing north.

*What are we doing? Are we on a sightseeing tour? Venezuela is south!*

I confronted Francisco. "What's going on?"

"Why are you so concerned about when we get to Venezuela?" he asked me, trying to be funny. "Haben Sie eine girlfriend there?"

"I really don't care when we get there," I said and added sarcastically, "It just seems logical to me that if you want to sail to Venezuela, you head south."

He saw that I didn't respond to his joke. "I have the safety of the boat in mind. That's my priority."

"Look," I said, "we have a west wind. If we can sail north, we can also sail south. What's the difference? We just have to tack."

I talked to Ulf about it. He didn't care, or didn't understand my logic.

For the next twenty-four hours we sailed north. The wind was still west.

On Tuesday, June 16, after two weeks at sea, Francisco said something about stopping somewhere in the Bahamas.

"Perhaps we should think of San Juan, Puerto Rico," I suggested. "At least it's in the right direction."

Ulf liked that idea. When the wind came around to the northwest, we were at last able to persuade Francisco to tack and head south.

During the night we had one thunderstorm and then the sky cleared. Morning came with bright sunshine and the temperature soared. The wind moderated further and we were, for once all three of us, in good spirits.

We did not know how far the storm had blown us off course. We met a northbound sailboat en route from the Dominican Republic to Bermuda and we came within shouting distance. Francisco asked for our position.

"Just a half hour ago we were at twenty-four north, sixty five west," the skipper answered. We also found out from him that the storm we had battled for three or four days moved northwest and had become hurricane Ann.

The storm and our erratic choice of courses during those days had pushed us far west, in the direction of the Mona Passage, instead of Anegada.

"That's actually good news," I said. The Anegada Passage, as I knew only too well, is between the British Virgin Islands and the northern Antilles. The Mona Passage separates Puerto Rico from Hispaniola.

"We are better off than we thought," I repeated to Francisco.

Ulf heard me. "What about San Juan?"

Francisco looked at the chart and ignored him. "Wir nehmen die Mona Passage and sail directamente for Puerto Azul, my home port." His excitement showed in the usage of all of his three languages.

On July 18, he got a position on the radio direction finder. "Wir sind now northwest of San Juan, heading directly into the Mona Passage." Enthusiastically he added, "Tomorrow morning entramos al Caribe. Then only four more days. Nur vier Tage."

We encountered more ship traffic, in and out of San Juan. In the evening we passed the port of Borinquen on the northwest corner of Puerto Rico. To starboard, Isla Desecheo was just visible in the distance.

Entering the Mona Passage, we met a banana freighter, en route from Guyana to New Orleans. At midnight, a tug towing a barge overtook us, bound for Ponce on the south coast of Puerto Rico. Before morning Isla Mona came in sight on starboard, a flat island with a lighthouse in the center.

We were in the Caribbean. A steady east wind propelled us southward. Our speed went up to thirteen knots after we rigged the staysails. I have never been in any boat at such a speed.

With the seas on our port beam, the boat sliced gracefully, almost elegantly, through the water. Heeled at no more than twenty degrees, it was an uplifting experience, compared to the storm that had harassed us for so long in the Atlantic.

Ulf was still disappointed. He wanted to stop at San Juan. "All this time without seeing a girl, and no cigarettes," he mumbled.

102

We left Isla Mona behind us, had a good measure of whisky and enjoyed the blue sky with a few puffy white clouds, a steady east wind and the smooth, long ocean swells—the Caribbean Sea.

The radio direction finder homed in on the airport at Maiquetia and the Dutch island of Curaçao. Seventy miles from the coast of Venezuela we passed between the rocky islets of Los Roques and Aves. A few hours later, in the afternoon, high mountains, which at first seemed to be clouds, materialized out of the haze.

To the east of our destination, Puerto Azul, are the towns of Puerto La Cruz and Cumaná. Two months earlier, Ken, Jeff and I had explored that rugged coastline as shipwreck survivors. The little town of Macuto was farther west. Macuto… that's where we stayed and had our last meal together, overlooking the ocean.

At eleven o'clock at night on July 22, we came into the harbor of Puerto Azul. The breeze gradually died and we took down the mainsail and the foresail. Puerto Azul is a members-only resort club with a marina and a yacht haven, adjacent to the village of Naiguatá.

With nothing but the mizzen, we maneuvered the *MACHETE* to the anchorage. While Francisco and Ulf prepared a bowline to hitch to a mooring, I steered the boat according to their hand signals.

After twenty days and six hours at sea, we had reached our destination, Puerto Azul—playground of the rich and famous of Caracas.

The stormy days of the twelfth to fourteenth had been tough, but were soon put behind us. The unpleasant atmosphere during the trip was something else, and not forgotten so quickly. Maybe things like camaraderie and mutual respect do not exist among paid crew.

My presence on board the *MACHETE* was that of a hired hand. It was a job, not something to enjoy. Ulf had never regarded it as anything but a job. He was not looking for adventure, fun or enjoyment; he needed the money. Francisco and Ulf understood that.

I was in pursuit of adventure and to enjoy sailing the wide open ocean. I was willing to pay for it. The difference of purpose had made our coexistence difficult.

Francisco and Ulf went ashore, while I stayed on board and made my last entries of the voyage in my notebook. They came back with cold beer and Ulf had a pack of *Phillip Morris* cigarettes.

In the morning Anita came from Caracas with Francisco's daughter, Nina. Anita had flown from Boston to Caracas the week after our departure. Francisco had missed Nina's graduation by two days.

Nina, at age fourteen, was a pretty girl. She seemed mature for her age and had a good relationship with Anita, her future stepmother.

Ulf and I helped unloading the boxes, crates and bags full of household goods Francisco had brought from the States. We made several trips with the Boston Whaler and loaded their old Datsun to capacity.

At dinner in the club bistro Francisco asked me, "Would you mind staying on board for a few more days? You have the club with all the facilities at your disposal. I give you two hundred Bolívares a day for food and drink."

I did not mind. "That's okay with me," I said. I was looking forward to some time alone. Obviously, he had already talked to Ulf and given him some money.

"Good. Ulf agreed to come with us to Caracas and help with things there."

Late that night they all squeezed into the car and drove off to Caracas, an hour and a half away.

I lived on the boat, ate and drank at the various pubs, bars and restaurants on the premises. Once I walked the short distance into Naiguatá for some local fare. From the not exactly hostile, but unfriendly looks of the town's people I gathered that they resented the affluence exhibited in their immediate vicinity. They did not respond to my attempt at friendliness, smiling and calling out "hola."

I decided not to venture into one of their eating places and returned to the club of the rich and famous, although I was not one of them.

Francisco came every day in the morning in the Datsun. On board we sorted out what would stay and what had to go to Caracas. We had lunch together and, without Ulf's presence, we got along well. In the evenings, he drove back to Caracas in the jam-packed car, leaving almost no room for him.

On Saturday he came to pick me up.

The road to Caracas joins the main highway from the port of La Guaira, a busy artery leading up the mountain. On the way to the capital of Venezuela, the highway passes some of the worst slums imaginable. On the slopes of the hills, human beings live in huts of cardboard and corrugated sheet metal, without electricity, water or sewage, surrounded by mud and sludge. The sight shocked me deeply, thinking of Venezuela as an oil-rich county.

Francisco lived in the penthouse of a luxury high-rise. The elevator stopped at an ample foyer. I entered a spacious duplex apartment on the twelfth floor. The enormous living room, dining room, den, study and modern kitchen were on the main floor. A wide, curved stairway led to the bedrooms on the upper floor. A rooftop garden terrace belonged to the apartment.

Francisco Hobel—I had discovered his real name, Frans Hoblowski, on the ship's papers—was a rich man. I expected him to have money, but I did not know he was downright wealthy.

In his study he showed me the model of a new convention and exhibition complex he had designed. "I wait for approval. Tengo conexiones," he said. "Sure el municipio will accept my proposal." He added, "My father and I own some real estate in Caracas."

I wanted to ask him about the slums I had seen on the way up the mountain, but at that moment Anita and Nina came in from the roof garden.

"I saw a travel agency downstairs at the corner," I said. "If I can get a flight to Quito or Guayaquil, Ecuador, I want to do that. New York can wait."

"On Monday we go to the Port Authority in La Guaira and check in. Without Immigration and Customs declaration you can never leave this county."

He handed both Ulf and me an envelope with a thousand dollars. "Thank you for your help bringing the MACHETE here. You can make your travel arrangements with Señor Avila in the Agencia de Viajes. Tell him, it's por mi cuenta. He will bill me. Ulf, you book your flight to Frankfurt." To me he said, "I pay your ticket to Quito."

Señor Avila made a quick call to Francisco and then booked Ulf on a Lufthansa flight to Frankfurt and me on Linea Aerea Venezolana to Quito.

I wanted to stroll along the main boulevard of Caracas, La Sábana Grande, by myself, but Ulf hung onto me like a leech. We sat at a table in an outdoors café and I ordered a cup of coffee. Ulf asked for coffee, pie and a pack of cigarettes. When it was time to pay, he had no Bolívares.

Nina prepared breakfast on Sunday morning. "I always do that for my father on Sundays. It's a tradition, ever since I was small," she said. "This time you are included. Aren't you lucky?" She really was a nice kid. Her English was excellent.

Anita assisted her in the kitchen, making toast while Nina beat the eggs into an omelet. Showered and dressed in fresh clothes for the first time in weeks, I watched them for a while. Anita had showed me how to use the washing machine and dryer.

Francisco was already working in his study. He appeared in the kitchen in a maroon, silken robe with some oriental print. "Good morning, good morning." He kissed both Anita and Nina on the forehead.

Ulf, the lazy bum, wasn't even out of bed yet. We shared one of the spare bedrooms. When he came out to the terrace where we had breakfast, he mumbled something that sounded like "morning" and asked, "Is there no juice?"

Anita looked at me, as if asking, did I hear that right? But she said nothing. Nina found it funny and laughed. "No, sorry. I can squeeze an orange for you." Like her father, she saw nothing wrong in the brash behavior of this arrogant bastard.

Ulf said, "Just peel it for me." No thanks, no please. I almost could not restrain myself. *What a spoiled brat. How can anybody be so arrogant, so unscrupulous? Who are his parents? Maybe they threw him out.*

Nina stood up and peeled an orange for Mister Asshole. I was ready to explode, got up and went inside to conceal my rage. *The people in this household must be the nicest people in the world to tolerate that, to let that punk walk all over them.*

Anita seemed to be the only one besides me who noticed his outrageous behavior. Francisco gave no indication that he cared. I thought, it may not be a weakness; maybe it is strength or a virtue to be able to tolerate such a rude, contemptuous individual. He talked about his project, that he had to go and see so and so, and that he needed to get in touch with his contractors.

"My father is coming over this afternoon. Nina, see if there is some of your abuelo's favorite brandy," he said.

After breakfast, I went out before Ulf could latch onto me. The city, at least what seemed to be the center, had a completely European character. Modern high-rise buildings, department stores, restaurants. No colonial charm, nothing indigenous. The subway of Caracas runs in a straight line from one end of the city to the other.

There were buses and taxis, but traffic was light on this Sunday morning.

I walked along La Sábana Grande, which I compared to the Kudamm in Berlin or to Fifth Avenue in New York, but twice as wide. I saw no poverty to remind me of the unspeakable conditions only a few miles outside this metropolis, on the slopes of the mountains.

Back at the Hobel residence, I picked up a coffee table book on wildlife in the Andes. It was that kind of a lazy Sunday. Nina and Ulf were playing a board game in the living room. They had left the terrace in the mid-day heat.

At four o'clock, Mister Hoblowski senior, a slight, elderly gentleman, arrived. Francisco greeted him warmly, his granddaughter gave him a hug and so did Anita. He shook hands with Ulf and with me, as if we were old friends. He spoke better English than his son.

He asked about the voyage of the *MACHETE*. "My granddaughter Nina insisted on the name MACHETE. She also designed the lettering," he said proudly.

Ulf brought to the table the pictures he had taken with his expensive *Agfa* camera. On the first day of his arrival in Caracas, he had asked Nina to have a roll of film developed. There were photos of us doing various chores on board. Francisco taking a bath dangling from a halyard; me on deck and in the galley; several of the storm. There was even one of my daughter Susanne, taken on the day she drove me to Newport.

Francisco showed photos of the *MACHETE* in different stages of construction.

We had coffee and cake. Mister Hoblowski served himself one snifter of *Courvoisier*, his favorite cognac. Limiting his visit to two hours, he embraced his son, kissed his granddaughter, hugged Anita and gave Ulf and me a sincere handshake, then he left.

I liked the old gentleman very much.

"He is still active in his textile business," said Francisco. That might be true, but there was a lot more to it. From Anita I learned that he owned a chain of department stores in Caracas and other major cities of Venezuela.

On Monday morning, Francisco drove Ulf and me in his Jaguar to the port city of La Guaira. In the Customs and Immigration building he introduced us to his friend, the *Inspector de Inmigración*. A clerk immediately took care of our declarations and stamped our passports, while Francisco chatted with the inspector. Business taken care of, we ate *empanadas*, bought from a vendor at a street corner, and drove back to Caracas.

"Franciscus, where is the German Consulate?" asked Ulf, who sometimes called him Franciscus.

"In Caracas, I think. We can look in the phone directory. Why? What do you want from your Consulate?"

"I know they give money to their citizens in need, to find a place to stay, to get back home. Things like that."

"But you already have a place to stay and a ticket to get back home. I don't understand."

*What he doesn't understand is how that devious mind works.*

"They have to give me money," Ulf insisted. "Peter can go with me, help me find where it is."

"Hold it a second," I protested. "I will be no part in your crooked schemes." I sat in the backseat, leaning forward between them. "What are you trying to pull, huh?"

"Nothing. It's perfectly legitimate. You ask for money, they give it to you. It's their obligation to help their citizens in need."

"But you are not in need. It's dishonest. You don't seem to know the difference."

"What do you mean? Dishonest? I don't follow you."

I realized this guy had no clue. *He doesn't know the difference between honest and dishonest. I can't hammer it into him.*

"Help him out, Peter. Maybe he is right," said Francisco, driving over a hundred. *He wouldn't know a con artist if he bit him in the ass.*

"All right." I gave up. "I'll get you there, but I will not go in with you. Once there, you're on your own, doing your dirty tricks."

In the afternoon, Ulf and I boarded a bus and headed for the German Consulate, located in the residential section of the city. We entered the villa with the German flag outside. Ulf approached the receptionist, while I waited in the foyer.

After a while, Ulf came out. "Let's go. They want to get me a plane ticket. They wouldn't give me cash to buy it myself. That's no help. And later I'd have to pay them back. What kind of help is that? Are they out of their minds?"

"See, they didn't fall for your scheme. You think they are stupid?"

"What scheme? They don't know I already have a plane ticket."

"Yeah, because you didn't tell them. You tried to con them and they saw right through you."

It was impossible to get through to him. He had no concept of morality. Defeated, but convinced they had done him wrong, he sulked as we returned to the Hobel penthouse.

On the morning of Tuesday, July 30 1985, Francisco drove us to the International Airport Simon Bolívar at Maiquetia.

I had booked the noon flight to Bogotá, with connection to Quito.

I checked my bags and said good-bye to Francisco. I did not know whether to admire him for his restraint or to despise him for his weakness. It did not matter anymore. This trip was over.

"Thanks for your hospitality," I said, referring to the last few days at his home. As an afterthought I added, "Good luck with the MACHETE."

We shook hands. "Have a good flight, buen viaje," he said.

I almost ignored Ulf, then turned around and took his outstretched hand. There was nothing I could think of to say to him.

The departure of his flight was two hours after mine. I have no way of knowing whether Francisco waited with him until boarding time. I have no way of knowing anything about their lives or the life of the *MACHETE.*

# Ecuador Revisited

I arrived in Quito, Ecuador, late in the afternoon. I had to change planes in Bogotá, Colombia, where all baggage was thoroughly checked. In Quito, my duffel bag and knapsack were not even opened.

I asked my taxi driver to take me to a medium priced hotel. She drove me to the *Hotel de la Real Audiencia*, a small residential inn on a busy side street in the center of town.

Over twenty-eight years had elapsed since I last set foot on the pavement of this ancient, historical capital, once a center of Inca culture. Palatial buildings from the days of Spanish dominance and narrow cobbled streets speak of two different eras. Indios—men, women and children—in colorful ponchos, felt hats and shiny-black ponytails share the streets with people in modern, western attire. Buses and *Colectivos*, overcrowded with passengers, raced down steep

113

inclines as they did twenty-eight years ago. All that had not changed since I lived in Quito in the 1950s.

Two things had changed. While the old Quito I knew had remained the same, the outskirts had expanded. With the modern parts added to the city, the population had increased to over 800,000. What also had changed—or so it seemed to me—was the climate. Quito, ten thousand feet high in the Andes Mountains, boasted of an eternal spring, but I felt cold all the time. I wore a coat, hat and sometimes even gloves. And now? Here I was, three decades later, in my shirtsleeves, late in the afternoon, enjoying the most pleasant temperature. At last the promised eternal spring!

I used to live in the Avenida America, on the northern edge of the town. On the morning of my second day in Quito, I asked a taxi driver to take me there.

The city now stretched all the way to the airport. Avenida America was no longer on the outskirts. We drove to the Floresta, where my boss used to live. That part of the city could not expand because of a deep gorge, beyond which the steady slope into the higher regions of the Andes begins.

To the south and southwest are the volcanoes Chimborazo, 6,310 meters high, and closer to Quito, the Cotopaxi with 5,897 meters. The Cayambe is almost as high. West of the city, a thousand feet lower, is the Pichincha, affectionately beloved by all Quiteños.

Quito is the second highest capital in the world, after La Paz, Bolivia. I soaked up the exotic beauty of this city and relived almost forgotten memories.

Then I flew to Guayaquil. My preference would have been to take a bus, but I could not spend so much time. I remembered the twelve-hour trip in a Land Rover through the rugged wilderness of the Andes I undertook with my wife on our honeymoon.

114

I took a room in the *Hotel Continental*. A port city of well over one million inhabitants, Guayaquil is the eternal rival of Quito; so different from the capital, it could be in another country.

Once again I experienced the hot and humid atmosphere, the peculiar smell of the city, the noisy traffic and the calls of the street vendors, the difference in dialect of the *Costeños*, compared with that of the *Serranos*.

Without the Indios in their ponchos and ponytails, except for a few working on the construction of apartment buildings along the river Guayas, this city lacks the quaint touch, the beauty, of which Quito abounds. On a flat, even surface, much of which was once swampland, Guayaquil is a grid of perpendicularly intersecting streets. There are monuments, parks and cathedrals side by side with modern hotels and commercial buildings.

The port was at a new location, remote from the city, where vessels are not dependent on the tide. The two most remarkable streets, the Malecon along the riverfront and the busy Nueve de Octubre, were exactly the way they were thirty years earlier.

I met with friends and members of Julia's extended families, most of whom I had not seen in all the years since I left Ecuador in 1960.

Again the vibrant pulse of this tropical port city engulfed me; again I felt the excitement the commercial hub of the country provides. But a city of this nature has its pitfalls. Pickpockets are everywhere. Robberies, even violent crimes are daily, if not hourly, occurrences. Embezzlement and corruption are rampant.

Three days after my arrival in Guayaquil, I boarded a bus for the formerly so adventurous journey to Manta, the small seaport. As I sat on the rickety bus, I remembered my many trips by jeep or by truck through the countryside. Although stretches of the highway were still in poor condition, unpaved roads, fording rivers and rivulets were things of the past. Travel time, then eight to ten hours, was now only three and a half.

I rented a room in the old *Hotel España* and asked specifically for the room I had occupied in 1955, my first time in this untamed, rustic town.

Manta, where I lived most of the years I spent in Ecuador, had been a dusty town with a population of 35,000. It was here that I met and married Julia and that our daughter Susanne was born. No wonder, then, that I carried a certain nostalgic attachment to this place, which by the time of my revisit in 1985 had grown into a city twice its previous size.

I worked at the steamship agency when there was not yet a harbor, and my duties included dispatching the vessels and their cargo. Barges carried the cargo out to the ships anchored two miles from shore. Coffee, cocoa beans and Panama hats were, and still are, the principal export commodities through the port of Manta.

Huge port facilities and modern container service replaced the old method of loading bags of coffee and cocoa from the beach onto barges. I remembered the times when longshoremen carried the port officials, me included, in their strong arms through the surf to motor launches for the ride out to the ships.

Originally, Manta had been not much more than a quaint fishing village. Now, most streets were paved. A broad divided avenue, the Malecon, ran along the shore and connected the port with the highway that led to the interior of the province. There was a modern five-star hotel and several first rate restaurants overlooking the ocean. Bistros were busy places on the beach, offering fish and seafood and the ever-popular *cebiche*, made of shrimp or raw, marinated fish, a local specialty.

The old days had vanished. Water arrived at the houses through pipes—no longer by tank trucks or in barrels on the backs of *burros*. Electric light, once sporadic, was now a matter of flicking a switch. The old landing strip for small planes had developed into an airport that serviced jets.

Yet, I discovered many a familiar house or building. The wooden structure of the Customhouse, the church and the *Clinica del Seguro Social*, where my daughter was born, had survived all modernization and growth.

I paid a visit to the *Registro Civil*, the County Clerk's Office, and asked for a copy of my marriage certificate and my daughter's birth certificate, documents I had lost in the shipwreck of the *HAPPY TIME*. The speed with which the clerk, a young girl, handled my request amazed me. In minutes she produced the huge books of the years 1957 and 1958. Then, however, the documents had to be retyped on *papel sellado*, sealed and stamped paper. I picked them up two hours later.

Of the German Community, once about half a dozen strong, only one member was still living in Manta. By visiting him and his family, as well as other old acquaintances, I realized the time span that had slipped past us. I would not have been able to identify any of them had I met them on the street; they said the same about me.

The days of retracing my steps, of refreshing old memories and reliving the past, came to an end. I flew back to Guayaquil. A cousin of Julia insisted that I stay at her house for the last night before my flight back to New York. I asked her to have lunch with me at the top of the *Hotel Humboldt*, from where we had a splendid view of the river Guayas.

In the afternoon I inquired about the price of an apartment in one of the luxury high-rise buildings that had the same view. While I could afford such an investment, considering the exchange rate of dollars to *sucres*, I would not be able to travel and live an abundant lifestyle. So, I gave up on the idea of moving back to the "country of my younger years".

On the morning of Wednesday, August 7, 1985, I went to the airport for my flight back to JFK, New York. I had rediscovered the country that means so much to me.

# VAMP

After my return from Venezuela and Ecuador, I again moved in with The Cat. It was not the kind of homecoming for which a wayward mariner yearns. I tried not to infringe upon her space and we made no demands on each other. We did things together or separately, and got along well for a while.

We drove to Baltimore and Annapolis on a weekend. She had fun pinning Crew Available signs on bulletin boards at marinas, dock master's offices and ship's stores. We enjoyed talking to people around the harbor, in the bars and restaurants.

In her small apartment in Brooklyn, the mood was gloomy. We were friends, but the lightheartedness, which had vanished from our relationship, never returned.

"I don't think I want to live with anyone again," said The Cat one evening, talking about the years we had spent together, first in the Village, later on the Upper Eastside of Manhattan. "Not with you, not with anybody."

"If with anybody, it would be with you," I answered. "We are older now, and calmer. Don't you think, we should be able to get along?"

I was not sure about that, and she did not seem convinced either. She knew there was this powerful force of the ocean calling me back.

Guessing her thoughts, I said, "The thing is, I still have to go out there again. I can't say no to the ocean until it's out of my system. The wind, the weather, the freedom and the adventure. The Challenge. Too bad, you're scared of the water."

"Peter, I can't swim. How can I go out on the ocean, if I can't swim," she protested.

"Who is talking about swimming? I don't like to be in the water either. I like to be in a boat, not in the water." True, I am not a good swimmer. I can stay afloat for a long time, but I can't swim to save my life.

"Well, I'm not going on any damn boat, and you know it."

I knew she would never go sailing with me. "Sure. So, we have no problem. You live in Brooklyn, go to the movies, to the theater, go shopping at Sacks and Bloomingdale's. You have family, you have friends. I have the ocean—not a friend, more like a temptress."

*I have to find a boat, I have to find a boat. I am like the Flying Dutchman, but without a boat. I have no place on land, I have to find a place on the ocean.*

In the days that followed, tensions mounted. The Cat and I got at each other's nerves. Patience ran out, tempers flared up more often, arguments erupted. We knew each other well enough to know where this would lead. We had shared too many ups and downs.

But, neither The Cat nor I wanted to part on bad terms. It was time for me to move on.

Early in September I drove to Newport, Rhode Island. This busy yachting town, center of all kinds of marine activities, including the America's Cup races, was a good place to find a boat in need of crew. Here I found the *MACHETE*. Here I would find another boat.

A few days after my trip to Newport, The Cat received a phone call at her office. A certain Jeff Bourne had given her a number in Boston for me to call.

Jeff was thirty-seven years old. Just divorced, he had bought a boat with the money that resulted from the sale of his part of their business to his former wife. Together they owned a kennel. The breeding and training of show dogs must have been lucrative, for Jeff was able to buy a hundred-twenty thousand-dollar boat.

His parents were well to do, but he was the black sheep of the family. The relationship with his father, a college professor, was strained. Jeff told me he had no access to the family fortune.

All this he revealed to me in the first half hour sitting in the cockpit of his boat in Newport harbor. What we shared was the passion for the wide-open ocean and the adventure of long-distance sailing.

He listened to my stories, from my Baltic Sea experience to the sinking of the *HAPPY TIME* and the voyage of the *MACHETE*. At the same time, he seemed to be distracted or nervous, always looking around to see what was going on on neighboring boats in the anchorage.

I asked him what his plans were. "You left a message that you were sailing for the Caribbean and beyond. What do you mean by 'and beyond'?"

"Australia. That's my goal. I don't want to come back here. That's why I liked the note you left at the gate to the main dock: Ocean Cruising Experience. Anywhere, anytime. No Time Limit. 'That's the guy I want,' I said. But we need a couple of women, don't you think?"

*So, this is what this is about. I understand. And the name of his boat… VAMP, a seductive female.*

"Well, that's up to you. A crew of four, then?" The boat, a C+C 40, had enough room, no question about it, but what sort of voyage did Jeff have in mind? I became a little cautious, a little hesitant. *All the way to Australia? I don't know about that.* I didn't know this guy yet; he had revealed something about himself.

"You have set a departure date yet?"

"I need a couple of weeks to tie up a few loose ends. My ex thinks she can get more alimony out of me. The lawyers are haggling over it and I have to be there. My father can pay out of my trust fund, which he refuses to hand over to me."

I really didn't want to know so much about his personal affairs. "I can't make a commitment on such a long-term basis. I definitely want to return to the US. 'No time limit' was not supposed to mean 'indefinitely'." After a pause, I said, "How about this: divide the voyage into segments. First leg, say, to Florida, or Puerto Rico or the Virgin Islands. Look, unless you have a childhood friend, or a wife, you can't find anyone to do the whole trip with."

"I know. It can take me years to get to Australia; I don't care. Even if I never make it… I just don't want to come back here."

"All right, then. No long-term commitment. You have any kind of itinerary?"

"Oh yeah. Bermuda, Virgin Islands, Jamaica and then to Panama and the Pacific. I have all the charts and guide books."

"Sounds good to me. Segment by segment." We shook hands. "I always wanted to go to Bermuda."

The boat made a good impression. There was a SatNav and a *Loran*, a stack of charts, VHF radio and single sideband. I saw sail bags piled up in the fo'c'sle. The C+C 40 is a racer-cruiser, a combination I have never been fond of. They usually turn out to be neither racer nor cruiser, but the Canadian-built C+C has a good reputation.

122

"So, it's settled then? When can you move on board?" Jeff stood up. "I have to get back to Boston."

"If it's okay with you, early next week? I can't stay too much longer where I am now."

"Sure. It will take me a few days to wrap things up in Boston, but there's plenty for you to do here. Maybe you find a couple of girls for us. I put an ad in *Cruising World* and one in *Yachting*. See what comes up."

We went back to shore in his inflatable. He drove to Boston, and I returned to New York. I was thinking about what he said: find a couple of girls. *Is that his number one preoccupation, or is he just talking 'macho'? VAMP—sexy, the eternal female, the bride, or the mistress.*

The following morning I stopped at Julia's house in Queens.

"I was wondering when you'd show up," she greeted me at the door. "I haven't seen or heard from you since the day you came back from Guayaquil."

I followed her into the kitchen.

"Coffee?" She asked.

"Yeah, thanks. Sorry, I had to look for another boat right away. That seems to be my destiny. A Flying Dutchman without a boat." I did not think it necessary to tell her that had stayed with The Cat all this time, and told her, "I am on a boat in Newport. Probably leave for Bermuda in a few days." Julia and I were getting along fine. No stress, no complications. Why should I disturb that?

"You better get your own boat one of these days. Either that or an apartment."

"I've been thinking the same thing. You think I will ever be able to afford my own boat? By the way, how's my money doing?"

"Let me get the book, it's right here. I don't know what you live on. Your biggest expenses are the phone calls."

"I got a thousand dollars from Francisco and he paid my ticket to Quito. My next credit card bill will be pretty high. Quito, Guayaquil, Manta. Hotels, eating out, and the air fare to New York alone is about six hundred dollars."

"So, tell me about this boat you're on in Newport."

"It's called VAMP. Jeff, the owner, is thirty-seven and just divorced. Wants to sail to Australia. Maybe I'll go with him as far as Bermuda or something like that. Australia? I don't think so."

"VAMP—que quiere decir esto? What does that mean?"

"VAMP. It's a good name. Means a mistress, you know, or a bride. Like the ship is the mariner's bride."

"Divorciado, huh? Thirty-seven? His boat his bride or mistress? He'll soon be looking for a woman."

"That's his business. What do I care? Anyway, how much money do I have in the bank? Can I afford my own boat?" *This subject of women usually leads to trouble.*

"Money? You're doing all right. Not enough for a boat, though. Maybe a row boat."

"Then it has to be the VAMP for now. If that doesn't work out, can I crash with you for a few days, until I find something else?"

"Crash? No sé que es esto." She had trouble with some slang expressions.

"Well, can I have the small room upstairs?" I knew I couldn't stay with The Cat much longer. "Couple of days or so?"

"What about your girlfriend? Split up again? She found someone else?"

There it was again, the teasing, the sarcasm. If we left that alone, we could come to a comfortable arrangement.

"Do we have to talk about that? Look, I can drive back to Newport today. It's just in case it doesn't work out." I changed the subject. "How are Carlos and Susi? Maybe we can all get together one evening before I leave on this trip." I turned around. "I'd better get going. Take care. I'll call you."

I felt bad about going directly to The Cat's apartment, so I drove to the Barren Island Marina in Brooklyn, where I had kept my boat, the *TRITON II*. I walked out on the docks, looked in at the office and talked to some people in the yard, just to kill time. The Cat always came home around a quarter to six. I had the key to her apartment, but this time I waited in front of the building.

She came up the block and I steered her away from her door. "Let's go out tonight, The Cat."

We had a table by the window in the Chinese restaurant around the corner. Our relationship was strained. The tension between us grew day by day. "The Cat," I began, "it's best for us to part as friends. This weekend I'll go back to Newport. I can move on board on Sunday."

"Peter, I have been a little edgy lately. I know that. I guess I can put up with you for a couple more nights."

"A little edgy?" I laughed. "You have been a real bitch sometimes! But I was probably a pain in the ass, too. Let's try to make it a nice evening. Cheers!" We raised our glasses of plum wine. "To the good old days."

"Yeah, all right. To the old days."

On Sunday I drove back to Newport. Jeff was on board when the water taxi dropped me off.

"I am waiting for a woman. She's coming from Connecticut. The only one who answered my ad in the *Cruising World*."

125

*Does he have anything else on his mind? I'm waiting for a woman?*

"Oh yeah? When is she coming?"

"She called me yesterday. Must be on her way." With some disappointment he added, "on the phone she didn't sound like someone I would be interested in. Know what I mean?"

I shrugged my shoulders. "I guess we'll be sailing with a crew of three, then."

He talked about his sexual prowess and exploits when, in late afternoon, Lynn Thordahl came on board. Her arrival saved me from having to listen to more of Jeff's bragging.

In her mid-fifties, Lynn was tall and athletic. With her handsome, slightly weather-beaten face and short ash-blond hair, she gave the impression of someone who is used to boats and the water.

I guessed she was not what Jeff had hoped for, but I thought she would be a good shipmate. In the course of conversation that afternoon, we learned that she had sailed on a lot of boats, but never owned one herself. A trace of an accent and some mispronounced words slipped through in her speech.

"I am Norwegian. Was born and grew up in Norway, but I lived for nearly thirty years in the States. After the war I was a flight attendant for the Flying Tigers. Later I flew with TWA. My ex-husband was a pilot there. Now he's an executive with TWA."

"Are you retired now?" Jeff asked. "I mean, do you have commitments? Children? A time limit? I ask because I don't have a short trip in mind. Not like a vacation or a couple of weeks. I want to keep going. Know what I mean?"

"Oh, I have time. I don't have to be anywhere. My son is in college and my daughter works for Norwegian

Cruise Line in Miami. I part-owned a restaurant in Norwalk, but I sold my interest to my partner."

All that sounded pretty good to me and Jeff also seemed to like her—as crew, that is. I was glad Lynn had joined us; we will make a good team, I thought. The ambience with Jeff alone on board was getting a little awkward. Besides our interest in boats and sailing, we had nothing in common. I felt uncomfortable talking about women and sex, and Jeff Bourne had not much else on his mind. With Lynn Thordahl around, that was bound to change.

We had dinner at one of the dockside pubs and returned to the boat for a nightcap. The evening was mild and we sat in the cockpit. Jeff and Lynn did not smoke, but they had no objection to me smoking a cigar.

For the next several days I stayed alone on board the *VAMP*. Jeff was in Boston, and Lynn had returned to her home in Connecticut.

I liked this town, Newport, for the nautical atmosphere. I roamed through the bookstores, the chandlers and the hardware stores and ate in the pubs along the waterfront, always crowded with sailors.

Tourists marveled at the yachts, some well over a million dollars, others mere dinghies, and they admired the classic, wooden boats in their slips. Only Annapolis on the Chesapeake Bay comes close to the maritime flavor of Newport.

Time dragged. By the end of September, Jeff still had not set a date for our departure. Lynn came back to Newport a few times, brought her gear and helped me with some preparations and provisioning. She was as impatient as I was. We were ready and the boat was ready.

Jeff showed up on Sunday morning, September 29. "We are leaving in a couple of days. Find us another girl, Peter, to sail with us?"

"I'm afraid not, Jeff. A guy talked to me the other day. I told him no. I knew you wanted a female."

Lynn said, "How about Annapolis? I am sure we find someone there. I know that town well. My girlfriend Andrea lives there."

"Then let's go. How does Thursday sound? If the weather is right, we sail out of here in the morning. Two, three days to the Chesapeake, then up the Bay to Annapolis. Okay?"

I called Julia if I could crash at her house for two days or so, and drove to New York. I brought four lobsters with me and in the evening we had a feast and a real family reunion.

"I have no idea how long this trip will be, how far it will take me," I told Julia, Susi and Carlos. "We sail to Annapolis. Maybe I'll be back in a week, who knows. Jeff is not... He's not the kind of guy I could be friends with, except for the sailing. Now that we have Lynn, it's okay, I guess. I might go to Puerto Rico, or the Caribbean. We'll see."

"What a life you are living now," said Susi. "You never thought you would do this. Nobody has a retirement like you."

"And you are what... Fifty-seven?" Carlos added.

"Yeah, a little strange, I must admit. From a regular office jerk to a bum, a vagabond. I feel liberated. I'm still the same person, but I'm doing what I wanted to do as a kid. It's all my friend Jürgen and I talked about. We rowed 'die dicke Vineta' on the Warnow and talked about crossing oceans."

*I must write Jürgen about this. He's a big shot at Bayer, doctor of chemistry. Will he envy me, or think I am crazy?*

"Anyway, you have the car again," I said to Carlos and Susi. Just make sure the insurance is up to date."

On Tuesday I had lunch with The Cat in the Sushi restaurant near her office. Two of my former Japanese co-workers came in. "Peter-san, what happened? I read about it in the company gazette. You almost drowned!"

His companion added, "No more sailing for you, my friend!"

"You will be surprised. I am leaving on another ocean voyage tomorrow." I never liked those two. "I am having a farewell lunch with my girlfriend, so... if you don't mind."

They shuffled along and joined a group of Japanese men at a distant table. "So, The Cat, are we friends?" I asked. "I would hate the idea of not being friends with you."

"Yeah, all right. Friends. When are you leaving?" *The Cat—none of that mushy stuff.*

"I get on a Greyhound tomorrow morning." I took money out of my pocket to pay the check. "See this money clip? You gave it to me almost ten years ago. I hope I never lose it. Made it through the shipwreck, went with me to Venezuela and Ecuador. I think of you every time I stick my hand into my pocket"

"Okay, put the money on the table. I have to get back to the office. Walk with me?"

"Sure."


Late in the afternoon of Thursday, October 3, the *VAMP* sailed out of Newport harbor. Although the weather was cold and rainy, Jeff, Lynn and I felt good about being underway at last.

We wore our foul weather outfits until we reached the Chesapeake Bay, four days out of Newport, and tied up at an abandoned pier at Cape Charles. Two days later, in gradually improving weather, we sailed into Annapolis.

Anchored in the middle of the harbor among dozens of boats, Lynn went to see her friend Andrea Varta. Jeff and I roamed through boat supply stores and dropped off the outboard motor at a repair shop for a tune-up. Jeff easily made friends in the bars frequented by loud, hard drinking boat captains and sailors.

That first weekend in Annapolis we met Andrea at her home. She and Lynn had been friends since their days together at the Flying Tigers. Andrea was Swiss and at the time going through the divorce from her Finnish husband, an oil company executive.

Her house became our home away from the boat. Always open, we had permission to come and go as we pleased: cook, eat, drink, sleep, hang out. Andrea loved the company and the unrestrained, impromptu parties. Her car, an older model convertible, was at our disposal.

Brigitte, Andrea's sixteen-year old daughter, had little supervision and did pretty much what she damn well pleased. She brought boys into the house, smoked and drank, and all her mother said was, "She's young; let her enjoy herself." The red Mazda TRX sports car in the driveway was a birthday gift she had demanded from her father.

Andrea's little white toy poodle was the third resident at the Varta household. Her older daughter, Yvette, lived in Norfolk, Virginia at the time.

"Yvette is twenty-four. She is a massage therapist and a volunteer fireman." Andrea had a strong German-Swiss accent. "Recently she had a motorcycle accident. Her leg nearly had to be amputated. She's just now recovering from her injuries." Andrea seemed proud of her daredevil daughter. "She is also a sailor, has a captain's license."

The captain's license, also known as a six-pack, is a permit to operate a vessel of up to six tons with up to six passengers up to six miles off shore. Such a license does not mean the holder knows how to sail a boat, row a dinghy or tie a proper nautical knot. I do not have a US six-pack license, but in my teenage years in Germany I had obtained

130

a class B sailing permit. The exams included practical tests from boat handling to coastal navigation, from maintenance and repairs to Morse code and safety at sea.

The description Andrea gave of Yvette greatly impressed Jeff. "Maybe she would be interested in joining us?" Jeff asked tetatively.

*Yeah, right. As if we needed a masseuse and a fireman on board.*

"I'll give her a call," said Andrea. "Perhaps she would come to 'Annapulis' for the weekend." She pronounced it Ann-uh-pew-lis. "Sounds more glamorous, don't you think?" She had a flamboyant, theatrical streak.

After a few days, we moved the *VAMP* from the anchorage to the Severen Creek and tied up at a private dock near Andrea's house. I washed the inflatable dinghy and patched a leak, gave the boat a thorough cleaning and, together with Lynn, sanded and oiled the teak toe rail. I drove to the propane station to have the tanks filled, and Jeff picked up the outboard motor. We went to Baltimore for an evening of bar hopping.

One day, when I happened to be alone at Andrea's house, Mister Varta came to see his wife. It was awkward for me to explain who I was and why I was there, but he seemed to be accustomed to find strangers in his house. "I stop by later," he said.

A few days into the following week, I called Julia. "We are still in Annapolis," I said. "I have no idea when we might be leaving and I don't care. We're having a good time here."

Another week went by. On the twentieth I could finally tell Julia, "We are leaving tomorrow or the day after for Norfolk."

I reached The Cat at her office. "Norfolk, Virginia, remember? We have been there. All those war ships? From there we drove to Virginia Beach for a weekend. Remember? Must be four, five years ago."

"Yeah, I know. We had lobster in that shack on the beach."

"No, wasn't that in Maine? Ogunquit, I think."

"What's the difference? So, what are you doing in Norfolk?"

"I don't know. We're not there yet. Probably just stop for a day before sailing to Bermuda. That's about five days at sea."

"Well, I hope you make it. Back to work. I'm at the office. You know that, don't you?"

"Yes, I do. I'll call you…"

She had already hung up.

We left the Severen Creek on October 23 at six in the morning and arrived at Norfolk on the third day. The weather alternated between sunny and cloudy, but stayed mostly cool.

The first night we had anchored in a shallow bay. The second evening we docked at a place called Deltaville, where we had the famous crab cakes for supper. As we sailed into Hampton Roads, a submarine came out of the harbor. All we could see were a huge bow wave and the black conning tower, the rest of it being submerged. It moved at an amazing speed.

Jeff insisted on taking slip at the Tidewater Marina in Portsmouth. Lynn and I took a ferry ride across the harbor to the portside shopping mall and strolled through the fashionable shops, food stores and eating places. When we returned to the *VAMP*, Yvette was sitting with Jeff in the cockpit.

Yvette was a robust girl with curly, blonde hair and rosy cheeks. Her muscular body seemed to strain under her T-shirt and jeans.

"Aunt Lynn!" she called out and jumped up. "I am so happy to see you." The two women hugged. "We are taking this trip together, isn't that great? Jeff said already, it's okay with him."

"Yes? Oh, that will be nice. Yvette, this is Peter," Lynn introduced me. "He came down with us from Newport. He has real ocean experience."

"You look like a sailor," said Yvette and we shook hands. She almost crushed every bone from my wrist to the fingertips. I tried not to wince.

*Massage therapist? More like a steamroller. I wonder how Macho Jeff will handle that.*

Lynn made a list of provisions and in the morning I went with her to the supermarket, several blocks away from the marina. A courtesy van drove us back to the boat with twenty bags full of groceries.

Yvette arrived with her duffel bag. "My roommate doesn't even know. I just left her a note: Gone sailing! She'll be surprised."

On October 28, we sailed out of Norfolk, passing in the afternoon through the Thimble Shoal Channel at the Chesapeake Bay Bridge-Tunnel. If this great achievement in engineering is not one of the Seven World Wonders, I think it should be. From Cape Charles in the north and Cape Henry in the south, trestle bridges extend toward each other, only to disappear under the waves several miles from land. In the middle of the wide mouth of the Chesapeake Bay, a bridge stretches with no apparent connection at either end. The connections are under water. Cars and trucks using this highway between the two capes travel about seventeen miles through two tunnels deep under the ocean and on the bridge high above the sea.

A strong wind from the north forced us to double-reef the mainsail and set the storm jib. An aircraft carrier anchored four mile from Cape Henry, seemed as steady as a rock in the turbulent sea.

A submarine approached the Thimble Shoal Channel just after we passed it. Other vessels were engaged in naval activities. For a while, a helicopter hovered above us.

With the setting sun behind us, we battled choppy seas; Lynn had a hard time serving us the meat loaf she had prepared while we were in port.

We sailed an easterly course in order to cross the Gulf Stream as quickly as possible and to gain distance from Cape Hatteras, the 'Graveyard of the Atlantic'.

My first watch was from three to six in the morning. The night was cold and the north wind pushed showers across the tops of the waves. Rain mingled with salt spray. My fingers on the wheel turned white from the cold as I struggled to keep the boat on course.

When the horizon became visible in the advancing daylight, I felt a warming of the air: the Gulf Stream. Jeff opened the hatch and stepped into the cockpit to relieve me at the helm.

Yvette was asleep in the pilot berth on the starboard side. The pilot berth is a narrow bunk above the couch in the saloon. Since the boat heeled sharply to starboard, Lynn slept on the same side on the couch underneath.

Hungry, thirsty and cold, I helped myself to some oatmeal cookies and a glass of juice, shed my foul weather jacket and pants and crept into the fo'c'sle. In spite of the boat's violent movement, slamming into the seas, I was able to fall asleep.

The weather moderated on the third day at sea and the *VAMP* proved to be an excellent sailing vessel. We steered 125 degrees, and at noon on October 30, we were 390 miles from Bermuda.

None of us had taken over the galley duty, and for two days, there had been no hot food or even coffee. Yvette began to share not only Jeff's watch, but also his bunk. A rift developed among the crew—Lynn and me on one side,

Yvette and Jeff on the other. They stuck their heads together over the chart, worked with the SatNav and tried to use the sextant, which neither of them understood. Gradually, communication among the crew deteriorated.

That afternoon I came up the companionway and looked back over the stern. Jeff was at the helm, with Yvette beside him. "What the hell is that?" I exclaimed.

"What?" asked Jeff. "What do you mean?"

I was nearly in shock. "There…" I stumbled and pointed over the transom.

Jeff turned and looked back. "Holy shit! How did that get there?"

Yvette laughed stupidly. "Hey, that was close."

"You did not see that?" A huge container ship crossed our wake from starboard to port, less than three hundred yards aft of the *Vamp*'s stern. "Too busy to take a look around?" I asked sarcastically.

Embarrassed and shaken to the core, Jeff found no answer.

I went below and told Lynn what had happened. "We can't rely on them, behaving like a couple of teenagers in heat. They almost got us killed."

Wind and seas increased the following night. Toward morning the boat was laboring in fifteen to twenty foot waves, foam blowing off the crests.

Jeff agreed with me to take down the mainsail. I went forward to the mast to release the halyard. Yvette gathered the sail and tied it to the boom.

The wind, estimated at forty-five knots, sent whole waves over the bow and back into the cockpit. For six hours we sailed with only the jib and then decided to take it down, too. Yvette controlled the halyard and I volunteered to gather in the sail. Harnessed to the lifeline, one hand on the bow rail, it took me ten perilous minutes to unhook the eight hanks from the forestay. Wet and shaking from the

135

exertion, with an excruciating pain in my back and shoulders, I took over the wheel from Jeff. He intended to set the trisail, a small, triangular sail that, when rigged between the mast and the boom, gives the boat some stability and steerage.

Lynn saw my inability to keep the seas on the port quarter and told me to go below to take a rest. After an hour or two, Jeff, Lynn and Yvette also came below and closed the hatch.

The trisail had remained in the bag. With the wheel tied down, the boat was under bare poles—no sail set. From time to time one of us slid the hatch open just enough to take a look around.

We huddled below, wedged in among piles of wet sails. Breaking seas hit the boat and tossed it about as if it were a chunk of wood.

"I'll have to talk to that girl," said Lynn. She sat on the floor, her back rested against the bulkhead cushioned with a sail bag. I had squeezed myself into the corner of the port bunk, my feet jammed against the table.

"You think that would make a difference? I mean, she's twenty-four, not sixteen like her sister, and even she wouldn't listen to you."

Jeff and Yvette were in the quarter berth. They could not hear us over the tumultuous noise of the crashing waves and the roaring storm.

"Their behavior is unacceptable, considering there are four of us in this boat." Lynn was angry. "She doesn't call me aunt anymore, did you notice? I don't care, but she has no respect at all."

"Things are not going well," I agreed. "I think the wind is decreasing a little. You think we could fix something to eat? The waves are smoother, or am I getting used to them?"

"I am not going to cook for them. Let them get their own. They don't share anything with us, hardly talk to us."

"Okay, I'll open a couple of cans, heat something up. They can get it, if they want to." I did not think it wise to create a deeper gap between us.

Lynn lit the stove and I poured the contents of two cans Dinty Moore beef stew into a saucepan, our first warm meal since Norfolk.

"Smells good," said Yvette as she and Jeff went up the companionway. "Save some for us. I think we can set the storm jib, to make some progress."

Lynn and I helped ourselves to a good portion of the hot stew and left the rest for them. Then I went on deck.

"I believe it would be my watch," I said to Jeff. "Anyway, you can go below and eat something."

They had set the small jib and the double-reefed main. I took over the wheel from Yvette, but she stayed with me in the cockpit. The seas had calmed further and the boat handled the eight to ten foot swells gracefully.

"What are you steering?" Yvette asked me. I guessed she wanted to make small talk, trying to be sociable.

I appreciated the effort. "Right now I am on 175. That's the best I can do in this wind. We need a SatNav position, to see how far the storm has blown us off course. Aren't you hungry?"

"Can't I keep you company? You know, Jeff and I are just fooling around. It doesn't mean anything."

*So, that's why she didn't go below. To tell me that.* I shrugged my shoulders. "I really don't care."

"I'll ask Jeff to get us a fix on the SatNav." She went below.

The wind veered to the south and decreased to twelve knots. We tacked and headed due east for Bermuda. There was a tear in the mainsail near the bottom batten pocket and we kept it reefed to avoid further damage. We could not use the badly torn Genoa and the storm jib was not effective in the light wind. Jeff started the engine to help us along.

In the night, Jeff urgently called me on deck. He had the midnight watch. "Look over there on the port bow. Is that a ship on fire? What do you make of it?"

Tired and alone at night in this vastness of the ocean, the eye can play tricks on the mind. I looked over the bow rail. Rested, though ripped from my sleep, I recognized at once what was indeed an awesome sight.

"That's the rising moon, Jeff." Partly hidden behind some clouds and reflected on the water, the image changed quickly.

"Is that what it is? Yes, I see it now. I swear, it looked like a fire. Sorry I called you up."

"You did the right thing. Don't worry about it. Four eyes see more than two."

I went back to bed. I had taken over the port side in the saloon, since Yvette shared the quarter berth with Jeff.

Lynn was awake. "What happened? Did I hear something about a fire?"

"It was the rising moon. You missed a spectacular sight. Go back to sleep; you have another hour or so."

After a fairly calm night, the wind came back with a vengeance. Jeff and I rigged the trisail.

Wearing her harness, as we all did when on deck, Yvette went forward to take down the jib while I manned the halyard. The bow dipped deep into an oncoming sea and the breaking wave washed her overboard. Lifted by the next wave, she was able to reach for the bow pulpit. Still hanging on to the sail, she climbed back on board. Undaunted, she finished the job and bagged the sail.

"I hardly knew I was in the water, when I was already back on deck," she said in the safety of the cockpit. "I scraped my arm and lost my wristwatch."

I had a lot of respect for her. She was a brave and fearless individual. A thought suddenly occurred to me that

138

I have never seen Lynn on the foredeck. Every time someone had to go forward to do a chore, she found a job in the cockpit or below. "I take over the wheel" or "I get this or that ready" or "I stow the sail bag". I realized, she has not even been at the mast, not even out of the cockpit.

The wind continued strong out of the southeast. After some showers, the sun made an appearance. I was able to repair the Genoa provisionally, using the cloth of an old, discarded jib and the following day I stitched up the main so that we could unreef it.

The seas continued high and our progress was slow. At noon on November 3, we were still eighty-five miles from Bermuda.

We made landfall by daybreak on November 4. By then the wind had calmed further and the seas were down to four-foot swells.

Approaching the islands of Bermuda, we motored around to the east side, the only safe entrance into the surrounding lagoon. A cruise ship, coming from the south, entered the channel for St. George ahead of us and then followed the markers that lead to the port of Hamilton.

Hamilton, capital of Bermuda, provides the main island with a spacious, safe harbor. The port of St. George is not big and deep enough for large vessels.

After a seven-day voyage, much of it in rough weather, we were happy to be in port and did not have the energy nor the will to add four more hours for the trip to reach Hamilton.

We tied the *VAMP* to the Customs dock just inside the Town Cut and walked the short distance to the government office to check in.

St. George is a lively little town. We came out of the Immigration and Customs building with our passports stamped, and crossed a small plaza to the White Horse

Tavern. Jeff and Yvette headed straight for the bar where they joined some tattooed and bearded beatniks. Lynn and I sat outside on the deck, overlooking the lagoon, the long concrete pier and the *VAMP* at the Customs dock. We ordered coffee and toast with ham and eggs.

In Bermuda, we were in a different time zone and had to advance our watches one hour. It was noon when we left the tavern.

Jeff and I removed all the sails from the boat and spread them out to dry on the lawn adjacent to the dock. Lynn helped Yvette inflate the dinghy and put it in the water.

After folding, bagging and storing the sails, Lynn and I went in search of a Laundromat. We found one just a couple of side streets away. Most of my clothes that had been stowed in a locker in the fo'c'sle were waterlogged and moldy. I washed those in a separate machine with a generous dose of Clorox.

The boat was allowed to remain at the Customs dock for up to five hours. There is no official anchorage in the harbor of St. George, but a few small local boats were at anchor on the far side of the channel. That location, protected by a promontory, proved too shallow for the *VAMP*. Upon advice from the harbor police, we anchored in the cove between the Customs dock and a crescent beach.

Bermuda's weather was cold and rainy until the sun came out on November 6. Lynn and I went by bus to Hamilton. Less interested in visiting museums and churches than getting a general taste of the city, I ventured out by myself. We agreed to meet at the bus stop for a five o'clock return to St. George.

I strolled along the waterfront. Deep inside the harbor, a cul-de-sac, was the anchorage for pleasure craft, indicated by a virtual forest of masts. I boarded a sightseeing boat for a two-hour harbor tour and found that the port of Hamilton was not a busy one. One single cruise ship and a couple of freighters were in port.

For lunch I had fish and chips and a glass of stale ale in a harbor side pub. Then I visited the fort adjacent to the city, a relic from times long past. The rest of the afternoon, I spent strolling through this very British town. Here gentlemen actually wear Bermuda shorts, which are proper business attire, worn with shirt and tie, gold-buttoned navy blazer, argyle knee socks with tussles, and loafers. Well tailored, they should not be confused with the baggy, unsightly Bermuda shorts American tourists wear on vacation around the globe.

Jeff and Yvette also went to Hamilton, but they had rented mopeds. While Lynn and I returned in the evening to the *VAMP*, they did not; they showed up the following day in the afternoon.

"Aunt Lynn, don't tell my mom about that," said Yvette. "She'd only get the wrong idea."

"And what would the wrong idea be? I think she should know about your behavior," Lynn told her. Yvette did not find an answer.

Jeff announced he wanted to sail to Hamilton. "Let's move the boat to the commercial pier for an early start in the morning." I pulled the anchor and stowed it on deck. We motored to the concrete seawall and tied up near the fueling station.

In the morning I got up at sunrise to be ready, but Jeff and Yvette did not come out of their bunk. "What do you think is the idea?" I asked Lynn. "Are we going to sail to Hamilton or not?"

She shrugged her shoulders. "I don't know and I don't care."

We went for breakfast to the White Horse. When we returned, Jeff and Yvette sat in the cockpit, drinking coffee. They did not say anything, and we didn't ask. Such was the state of communication between us from then on.

There was no further indication of going anywhere. In the afternoon, I took a long walk around St. George, separated from the main island of Bermuda by a narrow creek. I swam at Tobacco Beach, roamed through the old Fort Catherine and passed by Club Med, which was closed for renovations. I took advantage of the warm and sunny weather, but I had underestimated the length of my walking tour. With burning feet and aching legs, tired and thirsty, I stopped at the White Horse Tavern for some iced tea. Lynn sat on the verandah writing postcards. I was about to join her.

"Jeff and Yvette are busy refueling. Did you see the boat that came in this afternoon?" Lynn pointed over her shoulder. "Singlehander, non-stop around the world."

"Oh wow! I have to see that."

Tired as I was, I crossed over to the pier. Docked behind the *VAMP* was a sleek, dark blue yacht, about eighty feet long. Closer inspection of this beauty revealed, she had all the most modern equipment on board: power driven sheets and halyards; multi-speed winches; automatic reefing; wind vanes and electronic self-steering; wind and water driven generators; solar panels; numerous antennas and four cameras mounted around the cockpit to cover every angle. This was the maxi-yacht *AMERICAN PROMISE.*

Her owner and skipper, New England businessman and entrepreneur Dodge Morgan, was about to establish a new record in single-handed, non-stop circumnavigation. He had reached Bermuda in record time. Deeply disappointed, he had to put into port due to a failing autopilot. His wife and two kids had flown in from Boston to bring a replacement part.

142

Early in the morning someone knocked at the hull. "Hello, anybody in here? You have to move the boat."

Jeff opened the hatch. "What's going on?"

A dock attendant informed him of a big tugboat coming in. "We need the space. You can tie up at the end of the pier. That boat has to be moved up, too." He pointed to the *AMERICAN PROMISE*.

Morgan and his family were not on board. They had taken a hotel room in town. Yvette and I handled the lines and fenders of the *AMERICAN PROMISE*, pulling her along the pier. Jeff was on board, steering. It turned out that the *VAMP* could stay where she was.

Shortly before noon a huge ocean-going tug came through the Town Cut and docked at the seawall in the place the *AMERICAN PROMISE* had vacated.

The tugboat flew the Greek flag. Her crew consisted of seven Greek seamen, some of whom we met later at the White Horse. The captain, a pompous ass, spoke passable English and showed a strong interest in Yvette. Consequently, he invited all of us on board his vessel for drinks.

We were—at least I was—surprised by the abundance of liquor, beer and food, which they freely offered. Captain, mates and crew displayed great generosity and encouraged us to partake without hesitating or even asking. "The ship is yours. You are our guests. Do as you please." Such were the words and gestures of their hospitality.

When it became too obvious that the captain directed his interest solely toward Yvette, I felt increasingly uncomfortable. With a considerable quantity of liquor in me, I left the tugboat and Lynn followed me. The flirting between the captain and Yvette had become embarrassing.

"Come for breakfast in the morning," some of the crew called after us.

Lynn and I walked back to the *VAMP*. "Yvette is leading him on," Lynn said to me. "Did you see how she lured him into the corner? That old Greek goat had his paws all over her, and she wasn't holding back either."

"And Jeff laughed in drunken stupor," I said. "I guess he enjoyed watching them."

I did not know when Jeff and Yvette had come on board, but in the morning they were there, and they were in a somber mood. Hung-over, I guessed.

"Want to go and see if they have breakfast on the tugboat?" Lynn asked me.

Yvette had heard her." I'm not going back there. That man is a maniac," she protested.

"You seemed to like him," Lynn mocked her.

Lynn and I passed the tugboat and continued to the White Horse. There was no sign of breakfast on the Greek ship, nor a sign of hospitality.

"She must have teased him and then said no. That little bitch," I said. "I'm gonna have a Bloody Mary, first of all."

"She's playing a dangerous game, but she is a tough cookie." Lynn ordered coffee and scrambles eggs. "She has ruined the whole thing for us. We could have had free breakfast, lunch and dinner. Bermuda is expensive."

"Yeah," I agreed. "How long does Jeff want to stay here? I've had it, already. I'll ask him." As I said that, we saw Jeff and Yvette walking to the moped rental place. "Back to Hamilton again?"

"Probably." Lynn was disgusted with them. We walked back to the boat. "Let's take the dinghy apart and stow it away. We don't need it anymore."

We dragged the dinghy up on the dock, wiped it down, deflated it and put it in the lazaret. The poorly repaired Genoa was on my mind. I took it out of the bag and tried to improve on the hastily done patchwork. There

144

was not much I could do, but at least it looked better with a new section along the badly torn foot of the sail.

Another yacht came through the Town Cut. There was just enough room behind the tugboat at the concrete bulwark for that beautiful sailboat.

"That's a Halberg-Rassy," Lynn called out excitedly. The Swedish built Halberg-Rassy yachts are among the finest in the world. "Let's go and give them a hand with the lines and meet the people on board."

Dieter and Gabi, a young German couple, had sailed across the Atlantic from the Mediterranean, en route to the Virgin Islands.

"The owners expect the boat in St. Croix for an extended cruise through the Caribbean. We fly back to Hamburg as soon as we deliver her. We do this for a living. It's a pretty good life. The money is good, we have no expenses and sailing is our passion." Dieter made it sound like the ideal lifestyle.

"I sailed a boat to Venezuela earlier this year, but that was no great fun," I told them. "The owner and the other crew member were a pain in the neck."

"Ah, that's different. Never do a delivery with the owner on board," Gabi said and Dieter confirmed, "We don't sail with the owners, ever. Either I am the captain, or we don't take the job."

"Well," said Lynn, " I would like to take a look below. May I? How big is the boat? About fifty feet?"

"She's forty-eight. Come on, I show you," Gabi invited us on board.

We went down the companionway. There was a luxury I had not expected. Two staterooms, the galley on starboard, chart table with complete nav station on port. The saloon had a comfortable seating arrangement and dining set for six. The upholstery was in wine red velvet, the woodwork highly polished mahogany. Forward were the crew quarters, which Dieter and Gabi used as a TV room. Aft of the galley was the pantry with a freezer, a water maker, dishwasher, clothes washer and dryer. On the other side was the walk-through to the aft cabin. Gabi showed us one of the staterooms, decorated in cream and gold wallpaper, with sheets and comforters in a floral pattern. We didn't get to see the other stateroom; probably not made up, I guessed. Faucets and fixtures in the two bathrooms were gold plated; lamp shades genuine Tiffany.

"We only sail classy yachts," said Dieter, not sounding arrogant or obnoxious. "We don't bother with crabby boats."

Lynn asked, "How much does something like this cost?"

"No idea," answered Dieter. "My guess would be around a million, million and a quarter."

"Well, thanks for the tour," I said. "Stop by at our boat, the VAMP. But," I added, "You wouldn't want to sail in her!"

Later we met Dieter and Gabi at the White Horse Tavern. "Come by tonight and watch a movie with us," they invited us. "You like John Wayne?"

"Thanks," said Lynn. "We bring the popcorn."

"Where the hell will you get popcorn?" I asked her as we walked back to the *VAMP*.

"I don't know. We'll figure something out."

We saw some of the Greek crew working on the tugboat, others were at the White Horse but we did not see the captain. All hospitality had stopped, a total reverse from the day before.

"Let's go and see a movie," said Lynn and we went over to the Halberg-Rassey—without popcorn, of course.

Gabi put crackers and chips with cheese dip on the table, Dieter opened a bottle of fine Chianti and we had a great evening, watching an old cowboy movie.

146

After midnight we returned to the *VAMP*. Jeff and Yvette had not come home.

In the night, a strong east wind kept the boat pressed against the bulwark and we had to adjust the fenders frequently with the rising and falling tide. There was little sleep for us. Jeff and Lynn showed up as we had breakfast at the tavern.

"We have to get out of here as soon as the wind lets up," Jeff alerted us. "The water truck is supposed to be here this morning. Once we fill up our tanks we're out of here, if the weather calms a bit."

Glad to get on with our voyage, I did not ask about the sudden urgency.

Yvette told Lynn they had been to an Alcoholics Anonymous meeting. "That was fun," she said.

I thought, probably the Greek captain had something to do with the hasty decision to leave. My suspicion was confirmed when Jeff and Yvette quickly left the White Horse as soon as they saw the tugboat captain approach the tavern.

Lynn and I climbed a steep cobblestone street and went to the Bermuda weather station in the center of St. George. In the observation tower, loaded with meteorological instruments and charts, we spoke to an attendant who gave us a forecast of good weather for the next few days.

Before going back to the *VAMP*, we said good-bye to our friends Dieter and Gabi. Walking past the tugboat, we waved to some of the crewmen, but received no more than a meager reply. *What strange people, open their hearts and their home for us one day, and barely know us the next.*

"Where were you? Come on, let's go. The water truck was here an hour ago. The wind's okay, we can make it out of here." Jeff was in a great hurry.

I had noticed mood swings in him, but never before saw him so agitated. Lynn thought his behavior was typical for a cocaine user. I didn't know what the typical behavior of cocaine user was and where Lynn might have gotten that idea.

She said, "They gave us a good forecast at the weather station. High pressure for the next several days. Anyway, why suddenly such a hurry? What's the big deal?"

"We just want to be out of here, that's all."

At one o'clock, on November 11, Jeff started the engine. Yvette and I took in the bow and stern lines. We stowed the fenders and twenty minutes later, the *VAMP* passed through the Town Cut.

We were on our way to the Virgin Islands.

Our arrival in Bermuda was on a Monday, and we left on the following Monday. The wind was strong from the east and the seas were rough. Long before four pm, the island sank below the horizon. Our course was due south, on Longitude 66. Under reefed main and small jib, we averaged a speed of eight knots, climbing eight to ten foot swells, delaying for a second on the tops and then surfing down the front of them. During my watch the first night, from three to six o'clock, a thunderstorm brought heavy rainsqualls down on us.

There was no change in the weather for a couple of days. Jeff estimated the wind at thirty knots, the wave heights at twenty-five feet—both figures exaggerated, in my opinion. Conditions tend to appear worse than they are, which usually becomes clear with hindsight.

On November 13, I wrote in my notebook:

> *11:06, Lynn on watch, reported a flare*
> *(distress signal?) astern. Rose high, stayed*
> *for several seconds, left smoke trail. Jeff*
> *called me up. We jibed in rough seas,*

*reversed course and continued for twenty*
*minutes without seeing anything unusual.*

Doubting whether Lynn really saw—or perhaps
imagined—a flare, we jibed again and went back on our
course. Jibing is a tricky maneuver in calm weather, but
dangerous in rough seas. As the boat turned, the mainsheet
shackle broke and the boom slammed uncontrolled from
side to side.

Lynn was useless in moments like these. "Yvette,
get up here! Emergency! Get the sail down," Jeff yelled
out. "Lynn stay at he helm."

Jeff tried to get hold of the main sheet. I crawled out
on the boom, holding on with all my might, and gathered
the sail as Yvette released the halyard. Jeff at last secured
the sheet on a cleat and steadied the boom. I, however, was
far over the side astride the boom, with the crest of the
waves reaching up to me. The boat, rolling out of control,
made it extremely hard for me to creep backwards toward
the mast where I could get down from my bucking bronco.

The weather deteriorated, the barometer dropped.

"So much for the weather report," I mumbled.
"High pressure dominating this part of the Atlantic. Can
they ever get it right?"

Exhausted and in pain from my ride on the wild
mustang, I went below to change out of my wet clothes.

Lynn joined me. "I told Jeff I can't handle the
wheel anymore. It's too much for me. I must have broken a
rib. I slammed hard into the pedestal when that shackle
broke."

Jeff and Yvette took down the jib, locked the wheel
and came into the cabin. We were under bare poles, hatch
tightly closed. Waves broke constantly over the boat.

I insisted on one person on deck at all times. I did
not have to remind Jeff of the incident with that freighter

that almost ran us down, a few days out of Norfolk. We limited watches to two hours.

We had food on board, but no one seemed to be willing, or able, to prepare a meal. Crackers, cookies and candy bars or a box of raisins, was all we ate. There was no alcohol on board, not even beer. We drank water.

The atmosphere in the cabin was stifling. Tossed around by the violent movement of the boat, we wedged ourselves in as best we could between wet sails and piles of wet clothes. The heat, the humidity and the lack of fresh air were debilitating.

Yvette and Jeff behaved as if Lynn and I were not there. It was disgusting to see them climb all over each other, naked. I happily took my turn on deck.

Before going out into the cockpit, I faced the challenge of putting on my foul weather suit and boots, as the *VAMP* slammed hard into breaking seas. It is an imperfect art to open the hatch without letting a monster wave cascade into the cabin.

Hooked to the harness, I took my place on the helmsman's seat and looked around for signs of life outside our tiny shell. I saw breaks in the racing clouds and the sun peaked through for short moments. My eyes were burning from the salt spray. The sea was like a vast mountainous landscape with high snow covered peaks, valleys of icy blue-green glaciers. The breakers resembled avalanches as if captured on canvas by an artist.

I could easily imagine myself on an alien planet or in a prehistoric, biblical scene of doom. At times, high walls of water blocked my view to all sides. Then again, I was on top of crests and looked out over the endless, hostile element.

*Man does not belong here. It is sheer lunacy to venture out on the ocean. The ocean can kill you, if it wants to.*

In the afternoon of November 15, Jeff got a weather report on the single sideband radio. A tropical depression had formed over the eastern Caribbean Sea. To steady the boat, Jeff asked Yvette and me to set the storm jib. I worked well with Yvette. We managed to hook the sail onto the forestay and hoist it. Lynn refused to stand watch at the helm, claiming to be in pain, and Jeff took over the wheel.

The wind increased to fifty knots, with gusts estimated at sixty-five. We knew we were headed into a major storm. Seas mounted to thirty feet, and this time I did not think we over estimated.

Through the night we stood watch in pairs, changing on the hour. Sailing downwind, a rogue wave came on board over the stern, momentarily submerging me and filling the cockpit. The wave ripped my glasses from my face. Jeff found them as the water subsided through the scuppers. Yvette came out and I went below.

From my notes:
*Marine weather report on 16 November, 8 am. Tropical storm Kate north of Tortola, BVI, moving northwest.*
Later the weather station informed:
*Hurricane Kate moving toward Turks and Caicos. Hurricane warning for southern Bahamas.*

We were north and east of the storm, the worst quadrant. Rain pelted me, mixed with seawater, yet I preferred to be in the cockpit.

Lynn came out, tried to take the wheel so I could go below but soon gave up saying, "The pain is killing me." She stayed with me in the cockpit.

"It's better out here," I said. "I can't stand it below. Those two... practically having sex under our noses."

The wind turned south and I steered northeast, away from Kate. Jeff stuck his head out the companionway.

I screamed at him over the noise of the storm, "We should be able to avoid the brunt of it. I hope the jib is holding out. We're making better than eight knots, surfing down the waves." I was at the point of giving up the helm. "You come at the right moment. My arms and shoulders can't take much more."

"I'll be right out." He closed the hatch just before the next wave crashed over the boat.

"On this course, I think, we can escape the worst of it," I told him. He wore his foul weather jacket, and nothing else. I went below.

Later that day Jeff replaced the shackle for the mainsheet and he and Yvette rigged the trisail. The boat gained some stability.

"You know," Lynn said to me sarcastically, "this is a great crew. Nobody is seasick. Just imagine…"

I agreed. "The spectacle of their sex games is not as bad as if they were throwing up all over each other." That reminded me that we had not eaten anything for… how long? "Lynn, I am getting weak. We have to eat something. What would be easy to make?"

"We can fry some bacon. Lots of calories."

I lit the gimbaled stove and put a whole pound of sliced bacon into a skillet. Sitting on the companionway steps, one hand on the handrail, the other on the long handle of the pan, I let the bacon sizzle. "I don't like it too crispy," I said, took a few slices out and put them on a paper plate.

"Oh, I want mine crisp," she said. At that precise moment Jeff opened the hatch from outside and a medium-sized breaker hit the boat.

I had my bacon the way I liked it. Lynn, Jeff and Yvette had bacon soup, prepared in saltwater. Served with crackers, this was our first meal since we left St. George five days earlier.

On Sunday, November 17, the sky looked a little brighter. Either we had become used to the extreme conditions, or we were actually outrunning the storm. The waves were still enormous, but the wind seemed to have decreased to thirty-five knots or less and was blowing from the west.

We tacked and headed south again. Jeff turned on the SatNav. Under normal circumstances, we could have already arrived in St. Thomas, but we had 175 miles to go. With the improving weather, we set the double-reefed mainsail and later exchanged the storm jib for a larger one.

In late afternoon, the sun came through the thinning clouds. Hurricane Kate was moving away toward the Gulf of Mexico and we had successfully weathered the storm.

The last twenty-four hours at sea were fantastic. With the easterly trade winds of twenty knots and long eight-foot swells, we at last enjoyed what the trip should have been all along. We set the repaired Genoa, but did not dare take the reef out of the mainsail for fear the tear at the upper batten pocket might rip open again.

We arrived at the little island of Jost Van Dyke in the afternoon of November 19. Our CQR went down in Great Harbour of Jost Van Dyke. Yvette and I unfolded, inflated and launched the dinghy in perfect teamwork. Jeff handed the outboard motor down to me, and in record time the four of us were on our way to the beach.

'Fat Albert', the official on this island, cleared us in just before close of business. Minutes later he would have charged us a hefty sum for overtime.

Jost Van Dyke is not much more than a rock covered with green vegetation, and a population of fifty-three souls. The two-storied wooden Customhouse is the only structure worthy of that designation. Facing the beach, and painted in white with blue trim, it stands out among the huts and shacks along a dirt road.

We emerged from Fat Albert's office and walked to Rudy's restaurant, a hundred yards down the road, and sat at the bar under the reed-covered roof.

Jeff demonstrated how deep the rift between us had become. Yvette sat to the left of Jeff; I was at his right side and Lynn beside me. Jeff ordered four Piña Coladas. His gesture at the completion of our voyage surprised me. I mumbled, "Ah, Jeff, you don't have to do that." Boy, was I wrong! The four drinks were placed in front of Jeff and Yvette—two for each of them.

In the awkward moment that followed, Lynn and I ordered our own drinks.

A boisterous crowd gathered at a big round table in the middle of the restaurant. I heard German words, mixed with English, and approached the group. There were two German couples that had chartered a yacht, and two crewmen. They asked me to join them and the drinks flowed freely. With no real food for an entire week, I got drunk quickly and excused myself. At a separate table, Lynn and I ordered roast pork and yellow rice, the main staple at Rudy's.

Meanwhile, Jeff and Yvette were still at the bar under the thatched roof. They negotiated with some local characters; "for marijuana," Lynn assured me.

Jeff came to our table, already quite drunk. "Peter, who are those people you were talking to at that table? I want to meet them."

I introduced him, "Jeff Bourne, our skipper." After a few words in German, I went back to my table. Jeff, drunk and probably half-stoned, talked a lot of nonsense, made inappropriate jokes and embarrassed everybody, most of all himself. He waved Yvette to come over and they both sat down, uninvited and unwelcome.

"I have had enough of this, Lynn. I drank too much, I am exhausted, I'm tired. You think we can take the dinghy and go back to the boat?"

154

"I don't feel too good either. Didn't eat for days, and now suddenly a heavy meal and all this liquor... I'll go and tell them we're leaving." Lynn got up and, no longer steady on her feet, called out, "Hey, Jeff, we're leaving."

"Wait, we're coming with you."

We left Rudy's, stumbled back to the dinghy and motored out to the *VAMP*. Lynn climbed aboard and I followed her. Jeff turned the dinghy around and headed back to the beach with Yvette.

They returned at some time during the night, in the early hours before dawn, in a 'high' state of exuberance. "Wake up, people! We want to get going. Peter, take us over to St. John. You've been there, you're in charge."

Both he and Yvette were not tired. Whatever drugs they had used—it was clear that they were under the influence of something more than just booze—kept them in a wound-up state.

Lynn did not respond. I snapped, "Shut up. You're not in any condition to tell me what to do." *Is this mutiny?* I had already talked with Lynn and we decided to get off this boat at first opportunity. That would be in Cruz Bay, St. John, or in St. Thomas.

Jeff mocked me. "Oh, now he tells me I can't give the orders around here. I'm still the skipper." He and Yvette stayed in the cockpit.

"Let it go, Jeff," Yvette interfered. "They are tired, those wimps. They can't take it anymore. We can handle it by ourselves." Then they were quiet.

In the morning I prepared some oatmeal for myself and then took the dinghy to the shore. I did not bother to ask Jeff's permission. The telephone in the Immigration office, the only one on the island, was out of order. I wanted to call New York, let somebody know where I was. Now that had to wait until Cruz Bay.

Lynn had a bad hangover. She threw up several times during the night. I already felt better and put myself in charge.

"Yvette, get the anchor up. Jeff, start the Diesel. We motor over to Cruz Bay. It's only a couple of hours."

By ten o'clock we powered out of Great Harbour, the dinghy in tow. Both Jeff and Yvette were as docile as pussycats. They mocked me mildly, snickered around, but did not oppose me.

*Is that also an effect of cocaine, or whatever they were on?*

I was not totally familiar with the area and, sitting on the helmsman's chair, I spread out the chart on my lap.

Lynn came out. "What are we going to do? I have to get off this boat."

"In St. John, or one more night, in St. Thomas. Cruz Bay is nice, you'll like it. Pay no attention to them. We do our own thing."

"The wet sails and clothes in the saloon make me sick. I can't stand the smell anymore." She looked as if she were going to throw up again.

"I know what you mean. Stay on deck. Beautiful day, it's gonna get hot, though."

I maneuvered the *VAMP* to the Customs dock at Cruz Bay, St. John, where boats may tie up for the purpose of checking in. I left the boat in Jeff's care after completing our official business.

"Let them find their own way, you stick with me, Lynn." She didn't want to spend any more time with them. "I feel at home in Cruz Bay, spent a week here last April. You know, before the Happy Time disaster I told you about. I love this place."

We went to the little shack where I used to eat drumsticks with Ken Helprin and Jeff Darren.

156

"I can't eat anything yet." Lynn was still nauseous.

"I know. First you get a Bloody Mary. Then you'll see." I asked for two drinks. "She makes a mean Bloody Mary here."

I smiled at the jovial Island Mama behind the bar who recognized me.

"You back, baby? Ain't seen you for awhile. Where you been, baby?"

"Oh, here and there. Make'em good and strong. This here lady needs it." I nodded toward Lynn. "And then let us have some of them chicken thighs."

"Comin' up." She waddled away to where the chicken legs and drumsticks were hissing on the grill.

Half an hour later Lynn was ready for her second drumstick. I felt good enough for a Budweiser.

We saw Jeff and Yvette walking by. "Where are they headed?" Lynn was glad they didn't stop at our place.

"Maybe to the Junction. There's a nice restaurant. A little touristy. I like this place better."

We walked to the town dock where we found the dinghy. The *VAMP* was anchored in the crowded anchorage. I had no scruples taking the dinghy and we rowed out to the boat. We both needed a siesta.

Lynn dragged the seat cushions from the lazaret and made herself comfortable in the cockpit. I fell asleep in the dinghy.

The sun was low, throwing long shadows, when I awoke. *What if they wanted to come back to the boat and couldn't find the dinghy? Past six. Better get back to shore.*

"Lynn, want to go and take a shower? I know a place."

In town, there was no sign of Jeff and Yvette. We paid our two bucks for the showers and then went to a place where we had a Bucket of Shrimp—all you can eat for seven ninety-five, and a pitcher of beer.

In the morning we sailed to St. Thomas. Forty-five minutes into the trip we anchored in Christmas Bay. Yvette wanted to go swimming.

"Patience, Lynn," I calmed her. "Before noon we will be in Charlotte Amalie."

Her anger was about to flare up, unable to endure another hour on the *VAMP* with Jeff and Yvette. "If they come and inspect the boat and find drugs, we're all in trouble."

Of course, she was right.

To escape the stifling atmosphere in the cabin, we had to share the cockpit with them. We set sail for the last portion of this trip. Jeff was at the helm.

We had not noticed that Yvette was missing when there came a cry of "Yoo-hoo" from the top of the mast. That girl, crazy or bored, probably stoned out of her skull, had climbed the mast and stood on the upper spreaders, screaming in wild excitement.

Jeff applauded her while I thought of the problem we would have if she fell and drowned, or broke her neck hitting the deck. We would have to answer to the authorities.

Again, I restrained Lynn from losing her composure. "It's almost over."

Rounding Frenchman's Cap, the *VAMP* turned into the harbor of Charlotte Amalie. As soon as the anchor was down and the boat securely hooked, Jeff and Yvette dressed to go ashore. She had packed a small backpack.

"Peter, are they going to stay in town? What do you think?" Lynn asked me. "I am not spending another night on this boat."

"Me neither." I turned to face Jeff as he came up the companionway. "I'll go in with you, Jeff."

"Okay, then help me with the outboard."

I handed the motor down to him and he fixed it to the transom.

We motored in. Jeff and Yvette got off at the dinghy dock of the Yacht Haven.

"When you come back, Jeff, we will be gone."

"I thought you would," he answered and they walked away without another word.

I turned the dinghy around and sped back to the *VAMP*. Lynn was busy gathering her things and stuffing them into her bags. "How did it go? Did you tell them?" She interrupted her packing. "Are they coming back today?"

"I don't think so. How did it go? I told him. He said, 'I thought so' and that was it. We can leave now or tomorrow morning."

I knew there were showers and a Laundromat on the premises of the Yacht Haven, next to the hotel. "I have to do laundry, Lynn. I can't go back to New York with these damp, smelly clothes."

"I am not flying out of here right away. Are you? I am going to stay for a few days in the islands."

"Sounds good. You do that. I'll book a flight out tomorrow."

"Well, I've carried this with me since Annapolis. At the end of a voyage you must drink a bottle of Champagne brought from home." She pulled a bottle of Moët out of her bag. "That's the custom."

"That's nice, Lynn, but I have never heard of that."

"Whatever. Here, open the bottle. Normally, we should share it with the whole crew, but to hell with them."

We sat in the cockpit and drank the champagne from plastic glasses. There was something I had wanted to ask her for a long time.

"Tell me, Lynn, that flare or smoke signal you saw a couple of days out of Bermuda... Was that real? I mean, could it have been something else? A plane, a cloud, or a…"

"Oh no, I know what I saw. No one believed me. It must have been a rocket from a submarine, a test of some kind. We passed through the area. Who knows, they might have been checking us out. But it was definitely a flare."

I still doubted it. "All right. You saw what you saw. Caused us a big problem, though, with that mainsheet."

"That was Jeff's fault. He should have tacked instead of jibing, in that lumpy sea."

"True. Maybe he wanted to impress Yvette. Speaking of Yvette: what do you think happened with that Greek captain?"

"She pissed him off. First she led him on, then she backed off. The old goat got mad, or frustrated; anyway, she annoyed him."

"I think, she would have gone to bed with the man, but Jeff stopped her."

"Maybe. I don't care. Her mother is my friend. I'll have to tell her. Andrea is a little flaky herself, but she should know about her wonderful daughter. That little brat, Brigitte, is not any different, either."

We finished the champagne.

"Cheers!"

I got up and gathered my clothes to take them to the Laundromat. Lynn rode in with me. She went into town to find an inn or a motel.

We met later in the courtyard of the hotel for a cocktail. Lynn had rented a room at a Bed & Breakfast. I accompanied her with all her belongings to the B & B.

After dinner at an outdoor café, we said good-bye and promised to stay in touch.

"I'll call you when I get back to Connecticut," she said as I walked away.

The travel agency at the hotel had closed for the evening. Alone, I went back to the *VAMP*. *One more night. It won't kill me.*

In the morning I booked a flight to New York.

# The "105"

What would I do now that I was back in New York? Soon it would be winter and too late to find a boat in need of crew, going south.

My daughter had a solution. "Nick Van Horn is building this new boat, Dad. There's something for you to do. You know him; he's a pretty cool guy. I'll bet you two would get along great."

Nick owned the beautiful yawl *PETREL*. Susanne had crewed in her for a couple of summers. Once a contender for the America's Cup, the *PETREL* had come into Nick's hands when the Coast Guard sold her in an auction. For several summers she sailed in New York's harbor on lunchtime and sunset cruises, taking up to eighteen passengers.

I had often sailed alongside the *PETREL* in my Cape Dory, *Triton II*. Nick and the crew knew me as

Susanne's father, but they called me Captain Slocum, after the first single-handed circumnavigator.

Susi had started me in this vagabond's life by making the connection with Kenneth Helprin. Now once again she gave me an idea. Upon my return from St. Thomas in November, I welcomed an activity for the winter months.

I called Nick Van Horn.

"I can definitely use you. In fact, I need you. I have these young kids from the music school working for me, but I need a supervisor, an older person. I can't always be there. Now, you know, I can't pay you much. I am working with bank loans. I have limited funds. Eight dollars an hour all right? I pay the kids minimum wage."

"No problem," I said when he gave me the chance to get a word in. "See you tomorrow morning at the site."

The "site" was adjacent to the heli-port at the Battery, in the shadows of the World Trade Center. This large work area, partly landfill claimed from the Hudson River, was the place for the future Battery Park City. Mountains of sand, earth-moving equipment, cranes, piles of tubing and pipes left only a small space for Nick's office and supply trailer, and the maxi-yacht under construction.

On a cold morning in December of 1985, at the water's edge, I had my first glimpse of the *105*, a black, sleek hull, hundred-five feet long, supported in a molded cradle. What I saw was the beautiful shape of a racing yacht, but it was really just the thin outer shell, without the braces and bulkheads to strengthen it. The deck was already in place, but so far only provisionally fastened to the hull.

I had no experience in boat building, but Nick made me the foreman to work with a bunch of teenage kids, building a maxi-yacht. He put me in charge of a job I knew nothing about. I had access to the supply trailer and the

164

materials needed, and he gave me instructions for the day's work, which I had to supervise.

This responsibility was way over my head. From the six or eight boys and girls I learned what was fiberglass cloth, what was roving and what was mat; how to mix resin with the right amount of catalyst; the tricks in applying the resin to the glass, and how to avoid bubbles and dry spots, which they called holidays.

The construction plans specified where to use roving, mat or cloth, and how many layers. Nick stressed the importance of following the instructions exactly and he trusted me. Why? I don't know.

This trust, this blind confidence he had in me, motivated me to exercise extreme vigilance over the teenagers, ranging from age sixteen to eighteen. Most of them had worked on this project for some time. They followed directions diligently. Intelligent and respectful, they were nice kids to work with.

I moved into the basement of Julia's home that Carlos had vacated when he took an apartment in Brooklyn. My relationship with The Cat had corroded to a point where it was no longer desirable for either of us to spend much time together.

When I called from St. Thomas and told her that I would spend the winter in New York she exclaimed, "What? The whole winter? Peter, I don't think that would work."

"I know. Don't worry. I am going to live in Queens. There is an apartment free for me. But, The Cat, we can still see each other, can't we?"

The basement apartment had a separate entrance. I had the freedom to come and go without disturbing anyone. Before eight in the morning, I drove to work at the site, and came home late in the afternoon.

Working with fiberglass is a messy job. We wore overalls and work boots. To prevent the fine, hair-thin fibers from imbedding themselves into the skin, we sealed the pants legs and sleeves with duct tape, wore latex gloves and a hood. Still, fibers and resin found a way in. The gloves often tore and the fingers stuck together as if glued with crazy glue.

Although the winter was not particularly severe that year, the site had no protection against the cold wind sweeping across the upper bay of New York harbor. Working inside the hull, we were sheltered. Electric heaters aided in the curing of the resin and provided some comfort for us.

The most difficult job was to glue the deck to the hull. Strips of fiberglass, soaked in resin, had to be held in place overhead until the resin started to kick off, that is to solidify. At that point it was important to work fast and squeeze out any bubbles.

Standing on scaffolds inside the hull, two or three of us worked hand in hand on this tedious project. Dripping resin soon covered us from hood to boots, not sparing eyebrows and protruding hair. Overalls stiffened and, when taken off, were able to stand by themselves. At the end of the workday, we assisted each other removing gloves, tape and clothing.

The physical labor on the *105* was demanding. I have never subjected my body to so much climbing ladders, getting into narrow spaces, lifting bales of fiberglass or buckets of resin, standing on scaffolds or working on my knees. From eight to five, with a half-hour lunch break, it was a strenuous occupation. Added an hour and a half of daily commute, there was not much time for anything else.

I left my work clothes at the site. On occasions, Nick sent me to supply stores to buy additional bolts, wires, heating elements, acetone or fuel for the generator. For such trips I drove his truck, but on errands to the bank or the post office I used my own car, first changing into clean clothes.

I saw The Cat on a few weekends, drove out to Long Island with her a couple of times to visit her mother, or we arranged to meet for lunch in midtown when I had an assignment from Nick in that area of Manhattan.

"I don't understand you," she said. "First you sail boats, and now you build them. Look at yourself. You are a mess. Your face is all red, your beard is not trimmed and what happened to your hair?"

I didn't think I looked so bad, but perhaps I had lost some of my judgment. The Cat, in a midtown office environment, was of course always fashionably dressed. It seemed we were drifting apart in every way.

"I put on a suit, combed my hair—you should see me at work. Inside the hull its resin and fiberglass, working on deck I am in the cold wind that brings tears to my eyes. Its harsh conditions out there."

"So, why are you doing it? Can't be the money."

"Of course not. It's a challenge. I learn a lot about boats, how they are built, how to make repairs. This is temporary; soon I will be out there again. I retired to sail around the world. Now, that may not happen, but I will not waste my retirement sitting in an armchair."

Abruptly she changed the subject. "How's your wife?"

The Cat was determined to provoke a fight.

"My wife? I am divorced; you know that. I am fortunate that I have a good relationship with her. I occupy the basement and that's all. Why do you have to bring that up?"

"I don't want to talk about it."

*How typical of her.* "Well, you asked. It's a good thing we're not married. We would have to get divorced, anyway."

Whenever we met, that's how it usually ended. But then, "I'll call you, okay?" I still loved to be with her; we had too much in common, even in our quarrels—and she was so damn good looking.

"Okay, call me." She always walked away without looking back. I loved even that about her.

Often Nick asked me to assist him with the more architectural work. Together we measured, cut and shaped the foam ribs and glassed them into the hull according to the plans, to provide the strength the boat would need. With the blue print as our guide, we determined the location for the engine mount and he entrusted that job to me. In two days' work, I built the solid base for the big Perkins Diesel.

In early spring the construction of Battery Park City began and the *105* could no longer remain at the site. Nick negotiated with the Department of Transportation and the Port Authority for a new location. A huge crane loaded the unfinished hull in her cradle onto a barge for the ride up the Hudson. The new site was at the head of the pier where World Yachts Corporation serviced such mega-yachts as the *HIGHLANDER*, owned by Malcolm Forbes.

I continued working with Nick through March and into April of 1986. Before the *PETREL* returned from her winter storage in the Bronx, I helped Frankie, her skipper, prepare her berth at the Battery, next to the Staten Island Ferry terminal. We replaced the electrical wiring and the PVC water pipes that had suffered from neglect during the winter.

Almost half a year had run its course since Lynn and I had left the *VAMP* in St. Thomas. It was time for me to return to sailing the oceans, to follow the dream of my childhood.

"Nick, it was a great experience working with you and the boys and girls. I learned a lot, but the time has come for me to move on. The sea is calling me back."

"Peter, get your captains license. I put you in charge of the *PETREL*. I have Frankie, and Bernie is preparing for his license, but I need another skipper. Next year the *105* will be joining the fleet."

Cruising in New York's harbor, between the Battery and the Verrazano Bridge with a bunch of tourists did not interest me. The *105* would not be ready for another year, maybe year and a half, for her maiden voyage.

"I would love to some day sail on the *105*, Nick, and I thank you for the offer. But, you know, I still want to get out there, and then maybe buy my own boat." I gave him two weeks notice.

A week before I quit, a flatbed trailer truck delivered the massive keel and the rudder to the new site. I forgot how many tons of lead went into the keel and how many feet it measured, but I remember the rudder was five feet long, constructed of fiberglass with an aluminum core.

I never saw the *105* in her completed state, nor did I stay in touch with Nick Van Horn.

# CHANDELLE

Spring triumphed over winter and I became impatient. Five months had gone by. Sure, it was winter, but not in the Caribbean, Florida or the Bahamas. There was an ocean out there, and I was in New York City. Where and how would I find another adventure?

I saw an ad in *Cruising World*. Someone needed help to sail a boat from Antigua to Florida. There was a Boston phone number.

"This is the answering service for Mister O'Reilly. May I help you?"

"I am inquiring about bringing a boat from Antigua to…"

"Leave me your name and number. I'll get back to you. Mister O'Reilly is in Antigua. He wants a crew of three or four, at least one with experience. Are you experienced?"

I gave her the short version. "Yes."

Then I called Lynn in Connecticut. "Want to fly to Antigua? Someone needs crew. Seems like a short trip. Antigua to Florida. Interested?"

"No thanks. After that fiasco on the *VAMP*? I'm not risking another trip with total strangers."

171

She is probably right, I thought, but I was willing to take my chance.

Lynn told me what she had learned from her friend Andrea Varta in Annapolis. "Jeff is selling his boat and, get this: he's getting married."

"To Yvette?"

"No, but he asked her to be the maid of honor." She laughed. "Maid of honor! The wedding will be in May at Andrea's house."

"Who's the lucky girl?" I really didn't care. It was interesting, though not unexpected, that he was selling the *VAMP*.

"Someone from Boston," said Lynn. "Andrea thinks he's doing it to spite his ex-wife. Can you imagine marrying someone to spite your ex?"

"That Jeff would do that? I can believe it. Listen, Lynn, did you tell Andrea about her daughter and Jeff, the drugs and all that?"

"Yes I did, but you know Andrea. She made that hand gesture, like pushing aside what she doesn't want. So, I left it at that."

"Okay. Well, let me know if you change your mind about flying out to Antigua. Keep in touch."

In the afternoon of Sunday, May 4, 1986, I sat under a Tiki roof at Crabbs Marina on the North shore of Antigua, drinking a cool Heineken. There were few people about and nobody knew the *CHANDELLE* or her owner. I had a second beer.

"You mean Dennis?" asked the fat island mama from behind the bar.

"Dennis O'Reilly, yes. The owner of the *CHANDELLE*. You know him?"

"Maybe." She turned and waddled away.

Typical, I thought. Island people aren't always so friendly toward strangers. It started with the taxi driver at the airport. I asked if he knew Crabbs Marina.

"I drive a taxi. Of course I know Crabbs. That's my job to know where everything is on the island."

Well, maybe it was a stupid question.

That morning I had flown from JFK to San Juan, where I boarded a plane for Antigua. From eight thousand feet the islands appeared as if spread out on the page of an atlas. St. Thomas and St. John; farther north, Jost Van Dyke, then Tortola. In the distance to the south, St. Croix. Virgin Gorda and the smaller ones of the British Virgin Islands were distinctly visible, as was Saba. A bird's eye view of familiar territory. I imagined how the *HAPPY TIME* might have looked to the pilot of the Coast Guard jet when he spotted the wreck south of Saba, almost a year ago.

I resisted the desire for a third beer; it would make me sleepy in the tropical heat of the afternoon. "Can I leave my duffel bag here in the corner?" I asked the plump bar tender. She nodded silently.

From the marina dock, I looked out over the water. There were several boats at anchor in the bay, but on none of them could I see the name *CHANDELLE*, and I did not know what kind of a boat to look for.

After an hour I returned to the Tiki bar. 'Big Mama' nodded from behind the counter in the direction of a gray-haired, gray-bearded man sitting at the end of the bar, a beer in front of him. He seemed in his mid-fifties, wore shorts and an open shirt, gray hair sprouting on his chest.

Must be him, I thought, and walked over to find out. "Dennis O'Reilly?"

"Yeah. Have you eaten? They don't have anything here. I don't have much on the boat either." Then, almost like an afterthought, "Who are you?"

"Peter," I introduced myself. "Are you waiting for anyone else?"

"Two more are supposed to come. I want to get out of here ASAP."

On the plane I had some peanuts, and then a pretzel in the bar. I was hungry. *No food around here and not much on his boat? How will I survive this trip?*

"You better have a pretzel," he said and ordered another beer and a pretzel for himself. I did the same.

As the sun touched the horizon, we rode out to the *CHANDELLE* in his dinghy, which had a nine horsepower Mariner outboard on its transom. All I had learned so far from Dennis was that he had sailed across the Atlantic from Ireland with a young English couple on board. Dennis spoke with an Irish brogue.

The Union Jack flew at the stern of the *CHANDELLE*, a thirty-six foot Cutty Hunk built in England. She was a double-ended ketch with a teak deck.

The provisions on board being 'rather slim' was an understatement: a few cans of soup and tuna fish. We would either have to stock up somewhere, or make frequent stops en route and eat ashore. The latter would be possible if we sailed through the British and US Virgin Islands and then the Bahamas.

Dennis sat at the nav station in the roomy saloon, opening a chart. "You are familiar with these islands?" he asked without looking up.

"I know the Virgin Islands quite well," I said, "and most of the Windwards to the south. This is my first time in Antigua."

"Yeah, well, we're not going south. We head straight for the Bahamas."

"Sure. That would be the shortest route."

"Short or not short—that's not the issue."

*What is he talking about?* At that moment there was a knock on the hull. A dinghy had come alongside. "Hello!"

"See who that is, will you?" He continued looking at the chart he had unfolded.

*Oh boy, what a strange character. We aren't going south, we go north. I know that. Shortest route is not the issue. Then, what is? He argues about everything. This is going to be interesting.*

I took a few steps up the companionway to see who was there.

"Ray Kohler. You Dennis O'Reilly?" He climbed aboard and the guy who had brought him out in his dinghy motored back to shore.

"Dennis is below. I am Peter. We were waiting for you."

Ray dragged a canvas bag into the cockpit and then leaned into the cabin. "Hi, I am Ray Kohler, reporting for duty."

I bet he meant that to be funny. Dennis didn't say anything.

Ray was tall and trim, forty-ish and I could tell it was his first time on a boat. He stumbled down the few steps into the cabin and held out his hand to greet Dennis who did not even look up.

"Boy, I am starved," Ray complained. "They had nothing but peanuts on that flight."

"Yeah, right." Dennis finally responded. "I have some sea biscuits and a jar of salsa. Help yourself."

"How about some tea, then?"

"What? Now you want tea? What do you think this is here? The Hilton?" But then he got up and turned on the propane stove. "Look in the cupboard. There might be some. Pots are under the sink."

*Was there a spark of humor? The Hilton?*

We had biscuits and there actually was tea, but no sugar or cream. Dennis seemed to count every bite we took of his precious crackers. The salsa jar looked years old; I had my crackers dry.

Ray, from upstate New York, was looking forward to 'a boat ride', as he put it. "Never been on a boat. I climb mountains, I like the woods, the outdoors, but the ocean? That's a new one for me."

*He will have the boat ride of his life.*

I had stored my gear in the fo'c'sle to claim my space on board. Dennis had his quarter berth and Ray took over the couch in the saloon. We turned in early before hunger would prevent me from being able to sleep.

In the morning the three of us went ashore. The smell of food steered us directly toward the Tiki hut. A few men in work clothes sat at the bar, having coffee, toast and sausages. There were also scrambled eggs and bacon on a portable grill, which I had not seen the day before. The man doing the cooking did not inspire appetite, but hunger overcame that. I ate heartily, more than I would usually have for breakfast. When and from where would our next meal come?

We were still waiting for one more person for our voyage. I wondered why Dennis thought we needed four people to sail his boat from Antigua to Florida, with provisions on board not enough to feed a cat.

*The Cat! Should I call her?* I had not really said good-bye to her. We had a fight the day before I left for Antigua, but I did not want that to be the end of our friendship. It was Monday, so The Cat would be at the office.

There was a phone booth at the marina dock. I dialed the operator, had to give her the card number, the billing number, the number I was calling from, the number I was calling to, and then wait for her to call me back.

I waited for the phone to ring. It didn't. After a minute I picked it up.

"There you are! I have your party waiting on the line."

"Well, it never rang. Hello, is that you, The Cat?"

"Peter, where the hell are you?"

"I'm on the phone..." The old joke whenever she asked me where I was. "How are you? Sorry, I didn't tell you anything about this trip. I am in Antigua. Caribbean, you know. We'll be leaving for Florida today. See you in a week or ten days, something like that."

"All right. I'm glad you called."

"Are you, really? Really, The Cat? I love you for saying that."

"Yeah well, don't push it. Let me know when you are back. Gotta go. I am at work, you know. Ciao!"

That made me happy. I'm glad you called, she said. I could face the uncertainties of this trip, Dennis, Ray the mountain climber, and the food situation. Thirsty for a beer, I walked back to the Tiki hut. The grill was no longer there and no one tended the bar. Near the dock I had seen a soda machine and I was lucky to have some coins. With a Mountain Dew, instead of a Heineken, I went to sit in the shade under the rush roof of the empty bar.

*I called The Cat, but not Julia. That's not right. But that phone service here... and the midday heat... No, I have to call her.*

I made a collect call, had to wait again, and again it didn't ring. I gave it a moment and then picked it up. "Hello?"

"Yes? Oh, it's you. How are you?"

"I am fine. How about you? Okay. We will be underway later today. This Dennis guy is an assho... Excuse me, he's a pain in the neck. But that's okay, it's a short trip. I'll be back in New York in a week or ten days. Tell Susi and Carlos I said hello."

177

"All right. Take care. Hope you get along with Dennis. Bye."

"I'm not waiting any longer," Dennis announced. "He's probably not coming. Should have been here by now." He went to check out at the marina office, while I persuaded the bar tender to sell me two six-packs of Heineken.

At four o'clock in the afternoon, as Ray helped me get the dinghy ready to be hoisted on board, someone hailed us from shore.

"That's the guy. Peter, go get him."

The motor had already been taken off the dinghy. I had to row.

A big man, well over six feet and in the vicinity of 250 pounds, waved to me as I approached the dock. He was young, mid-thirties, I guessed. His red T-shirt, white shorts and Sperry topsiders did not help to disguise him as a sailor.

Carelessly he threw his backpack into the dinghy but did not let go of his black leather briefcase—a young business executive, who tried to act as he expected a sailor would act. Heavily, and with an uncertain step, he lowered himself into the dinghy.

"Lambertus de Boer." He held his hand out. A friendly, jovial type, he would change the stuffy, awkward ambiance on board. I sensed I could become friends with him. Notwithstanding his formal briefcase, he gave the impression he had come to have a good time.

"Peter," I said shaking his hand. "We were just about to leave when you showed up. A few moments later you would have missed the boat. Dennis O'Reilly didn't want to wait any longer. You'll meet him in a minute."

"I can't wait."

With the added weight it was a lot harder to row. "And then there is Ray," I said. "From upstate New York. Where are you from?"

178

"Montreal. I am a financial advisor in a big investment company." He was a little too proud of himself, but not without humor.

"What do your friends call you? Bert?"

"No. They call me Lambertus," he answered with a big smile. He wore expensive glasses with a thin gold frame.

The Diesel was running when we arrived at the *CHANDELLE*. Dennis was on the foredeck, preparing to raise the anchor. Ray stood helplessly in the cockpit, not knowing what to do.

"Lambertus de Boer," I introduced him.

"About time." Dennis did not interrupt his work with the anchor chain. "You know anything about boats?"

"Not much," Lambertus said, again with that big smile.

"Good. You can take off the sail covers."

Ray helped us take off the covers and fold them. The *CHANDELLE* had brown sails, like those of the *MACHETE*.

The anchor on deck, Dennis put the engine in gear and steered out of the anchorage. We toasted to the beginning of our voyage, clicking bottles, as we left Antigua behind.

Dennis made a weak attempt at cheerfulness. *Might there be a seed of good humor behind that unrelenting haughtiness?*

Night came, and with nothing to do, Ray went below to get some sleep. "Wake me if there is something interesting."

Lambertus and I remained in the cockpit. Dennis spent most of the night at the nav station. He had given me the course to steer for St. Barts. As usual the first night at sea, I did not feel the need for sleep and I took over the midnight watch.

The wind was east at ten to fifteen knots. There was one squall before morning. I wore my lightweight foul weather jacket and Lambertus donned a red slicker—brand new, it seemed to me.

At eight the following morning, we anchored in the harbor of Gustavia, the principal port on the little French island of St. Barts. The official at the Customhouse performed his duty with French peculiarity rather than in island leisure.

St. Barts was like a miniature Martinique, with neat houses and clean streets. We went to a beach of fine white sand, drank Kronenberg beer brewed in Strasbourg, and in the evening we had dinner in a French restaurant. The waiter showed us beautiful specimen of live lobsters to chose from, but what came to the table were not the ones we had selected. With years in the seafood business behind me, I detected 'freezer burn' in my previously frozen crustacean. Drinking much wine and having a good time, we did not want to spoil the mood by complaining over so trivial an incident and enjoyed our meal. Even Dennis seemed less petulant.

Dennis announced we were sailing to Saba, the little Dutch island in the middle of the Anegada Passage. I was ecstatic. It was almost exactly one year since the *HAPPY TIME V* disaster, just thirty miles south of Saba.

In the morning we sailed out of Gustavia. The wind was light, except for some gusts in squalls. Lambertus had his first turn at the helm and he kept the compass needle meticulously 240 degrees. The four of us were in the cockpit and I debated with myself: should I tell them my tale of the *HAPPY TIME V*? I went below and took four bottles of Heineken from the icebox.

"One year ago, in these exact waters, I was in a boat called the *HAPPY TIME V*," I began. "She was an old trimaran. At four o'clock in the afternoon she lost her keel and sank."

I paused to see if I should go on. Dennis pretended not to be interested. Ray and Lambertus wanted to hear more, expecting an old sailor's yarn.

Abbreviating the story, I ended with "We were rescued by the freighter *PACIFIC FREEDOM* and ended up in Cumaná, Venezuela."

"Wow! What happened then?" Ray was fascinated.

"We had lost everything. An incredible feeling, to have nothing but your life." Again I found it difficult to explain the lightness, the euphoria that came over us as we set foot on solid ground.

My tale had impressed Ray the most. He nodded, pensive and sympathetic. Only he seemed to understand.

Dennis asked, skeptically, "And that happened right here, last year?"

"Thirty miles south of Saba, one year ago, day after tomorrow."

Lambertus thought is was a fun story. "Let's see if there is any debris, Peter. Maybe we find your duffel bag floating around here." He pretended to search the ocean. "There, yes, I think I see something. Way over to port." Then he saw that I was lost in the memory. "Sorry, must have been not so much fun for you."

I regretted having told them. *Some things you just can't tell and expect people to understand.*

The heavy Cutty Hunk moved sluggishly in the light breeze, under main, jib and mizzen. We needed seven hours to cover the short distance from St. Barts to Saba, isolated in the Anegada Passage.

The French and the English occupied the island briefly in the seventeenth century. The Dutch took possession of Saba in 1816, and it remains Dutch to this day, although the principal language is English.

Saba fishermen are said to be among the world's best seamen. As there are no beaches and no natural harbor, it required special skill to launch or land a craft until a breakwater was built to protect a small basin at the southwestern corner. The island is a rock rising straight from the ocean, with two main peaks, the highest of about 2,870 feet.

The permanent population is just over one thousand and there is but one road for vehicular traffic, connecting the few settlements. Most other roads are steep footpaths. Orientation is easy, as the bottom is called The Bottom; the windward side is The Windward Side; the highest peak is The Mountain, and the steep ascent to The Great Hill is The Ladder. On the Westside is the Hot Water Spring. In the northeast, there is room for a landing strip for small planes.

Sailing around the head of the jetty, the *CHANDELLE* came into the calm waters behind the breakwater and we docked at a wooden pier. A Dutch Customs official welcomed us to the island.

We found a little café at the foot of The Summit, another appropriately named peak. Although it was a sunny day, the air was cool and coffee or hot tea suited us better than beer. The proprietor told us that liquor was available only at a few places and that alcohol consumption was very low. That may be one of the reasons that there is no crime on Saba.

Ray wanted to walk up the 1,069 steps to The Summit, but he found no one among us to accompany him. Besides, Dennis was not inclined to spend the night on the island.

We sailed at six in the evening. Dennis had decided to sail via the Virgin Islands, after all. He charted a course of 305 degrees, about northwest, that would take us south of Virgin Gorda and the rest of the British islands.

The wind was unusually calm, the sea gently rolling with one or two foot swells. The CHANDELLE, moving in slow motion, allowed us to relax and even take a swim,

182

tethered to our harnesses. Lambertus had bought some wine and food in Gustavia and we feasted on French bread, Camembert and pâté, and a good bottle of Bordeaux.

I slept until three in the morning when Ray woke me for my turn to stand watch. Dennis had been less pugnacious since our visit to St. Barts, so I tried to persuade him to sail through Sir Frances Drake Channel.

"The trip would be more interesting," I argued. "We could stop at Virgin Gorda, see Tortola and some of the other little islands."

I met with his resistance. "This is not a sightseeing trip. We are taking the boat to Florida. That's what you are here for." He was again his old self.

*What then was St. Bart and Saba, if not sightseeing?*

His snappy answer angered Ray. "I embarked on this adventure as a vacation. You make it as if it were forced labor. You think you can boss us around?"

"You can get off the boat, if you don't like it."

"Maybe I will," Ray hurled back at him.

Lambertus grinned. He was still amused, but this was getting ugly. Although no more was said, the rift between Dennis and Ray had become irreparable.

During the second night, we sailed past the south sides of Ginger, Salt and Norman's Island.

I dared make another suggestion. "Dennis, we could go into Cruz Bay on St. John. It's so much easier and faster to clear Customs there instead of Charlotte Amalie. It's also a good place to stock up on provisions."

He, of course, rejected that idea. "We go into Charlotte Amalie, and that's it. Like it or not." There was no reasoning with that man.

We closed in on St. Thomas and shortly after daybreak we entered the harbor of Charlotte Amalie. At anchor near the Yacht Haven, we launched the dinghy and attached the Mariner outboard motor to the transom. It was still too early to go to the offices of Customs and Immigration.

"I am going ashore to take a shower and have breakfast. Who wants to come with me?" I made it clear that I would use the dinghy without asking, if there were no other priorities.

This caught Dennis by surprise. After a moment of consternation, he put himself back in charge. "We all go in. Bring your passports. Come on, let's go."

Ray had not forgotten the exchange of words he and Dennis had earlier. "You are acting like a drill sergeant," he spat out. "You think we are your recruits?"

"You don't like it, get the hell of my boat."

It was the last straw. Ray grabbed his bag, which he had already packed. "Not a minute too soon."

In silence we motored to the dinghy dock of the Yacht Haven. I walked straight to the showers, while the others sat down in front of the snack bar. When I came back, Dennis and Lambertus finished their coffee and went to the showers.

Ray and I were alone. At the counter I got coffee for both of us. "Are you really getting off here? Think about it, you wanted to try out something other than mountain climbing and do a little sailing. Don't let him ruin that for you."

"That man is a tyrant."

"Sure, he's an asshole."

"Nobody treats me like that." Ray was adamant. "I'm not going back on that boat."

A delivery boy brought a basket of fresh Danish and I got up to get us a couple of them when Dennis and Lambertus rejoined us. Lambertus came over to the counter to help me carry coffee and the Danish to the table.

"Is Ray leaving?" he whispered to me.

I nodded.

The sun was already beating down on us when we walked along the harbor front to the Customs office.

"Would have been so easy in Cruz Bay," I said. "It's a long walk, almost to French Town, at least twenty minutes."

Dennis heard me, but did not respond.

Sweating in the morning heat, we stood in line for half an hour. "In Cruz Bay we would have been in and out in no time," I taunted Dennis. Again he said nothing.

Once processed at Customs, we had to walk to the Government Building.

"In Cruz Bay everything is in the same place," I said to Lambertus.

"You hear that, Dennis? We should have checked in at Cruz Bay, as Peter told you."

"I know what I'm doing." He would never admit a mistake.

The Immigration Department was on the second floor. Lambertus had removed his shirt in the rising heat.

"You must wear shoes and shirt in the Government Building," a guard told him as we climbed the stairs.

"Yeah, Lambertus, show some respect," I teased him.

Back at the snack bar of the marina, Ray recovered his bag, which he had left behind the counter.

He put a slip of paper on the table between Lambertus and me. "I'm off to the airport. Here's my address and phone number. Maybe we get in touch some time."

He and Dennis ignored each other. Ray picked up his canvas bag, said, "so long" and walked away to the street to find a cab. His leaving was rather unceremoniously and neither Lambertus nor I felt a great loss.

"They could have settled their grievances differently," Lambertus said to me after Dennis left the table to return to the boat. "Ray was nearly as hard to take as Dennis."

"Right," I agreed. "Want to go into town, see Charlotte Amalie?"

"Sure, let's go."

"I'll be your tour guide. I've been here before. Come on."

We walked into the center of town, ate rice and beans with roast pork and plantains in a noisy, dingy restaurant. Lambertus was a good sport, with an interest in local habits. It was Friday afternoon and some celebration was underway. The sound of steel drums and a marching band attracted us. Crowds had gathered in the narrow streets of downtown.

Tourists mingled with Rastafarians. Children ran ahead of colorful floats. Cars and motorbikes, horns blasting, cleared the way for the parade. Boys and girls in school uniforms, with drums and fifes, followed the steel drum band. Clowns and twenty-foot giants on stilts entertained the crowd. We did not find out the reason for the festivities, but it looked like carnival.

Thirsty, with dry throats from the heat, the dust and the screaming over the din in the confusion of noises, we found a patio bar in a side street. The fiesta continued, but we were glad to sit and refresh ourselves with a couple of Heinekens.

Reluctant to return to the *CHANDELLE*, to face dull and humorless Dennis, we spent hours in different bars and walked through shops that advertised duty-free cameras, jewelry and perfumes. I restrained Lambertus from buying stuff he didn't need and could find at better prices in Canada or the States.

Evening came and we headed back to the Yacht Haven. The dinghy was not there. We had one more beer by the hotel pool and found someone willing to give us a ride out to the *CHANDELLE*.

186

Dennis was on board, sitting at the nav station.

"Hey Dennis, did you have a good time in Charlotte Amalie?" Lambertus asked him, going down into the cabin. "There was a carnival parade. Steel drums, marching bands. Lots of beer. So, what did you do? Had a good time?" He was obviously taunting him.

"Depends, what you call a good time." *Typical Dennis. Sour, bitter, unimaginative, jaded, dull, opposed to everything—whatever describes him best.*

I stayed in the cockpit. Lambertus came back out, making a face, ridiculing Dennis. We ate crackers with the rest of the cheese he had bought in St. Barts.

"No thanks. No wine for me. "I waved my hand refusing the glass he held out to me. "I must have had at least half a dozen beers."

Dennis announced, "Tomorrow morning we tie up at the fuel dock to take Diesel and water. Then we leave for the States." He turned back to the chart he had been studying. Over his shoulder he said, "Take the dinghy on board. We don't need it anymore."

"Tonight?" Lambertus asked, mockingly. "This is leisure time. We do it in the morning."

The dinghy had its place on the foredeck. It was a big job to remove the motor from the transom, lift it on board and then hoist the dinghy with the halyard.

"Early in the morning, then. I want to get underway before ten." Dennis did not order us around the way he did with Ray. Those two had been incompatible right from the start. Since Ray had jumped ship, the atmosphere was somewhat lighter. Lambertus and I formed an alliance of sorts, and Dennis was careful not to step on our toes.

In the morning we stowed the dinghy, refueled and sailed out of St. Thomas.

Saturday, May 10, was a rainy day. A good south wind hurried us toward Culebra, the small island between St. Thomas and Puerto Rico.

A thunderstorm came down on us as we docked at the short commercial pier in Dewey. Rain continued throughout the afternoon and evening. We went ashore and walked up a muddy road to find a restaurant, a pub or a bar, anything to get us out of the rain. With hardly any provisions on board, we depended on shore visits.

On our way we passed some houses, but nobody was out on the street. The weather kept people at home. A man and a woman sat comfortably in wicker chairs under the roof of a screened porch. We waved "hello", water dripping from our vinyl jackets and hoods.

"Out for a walk in the rain? It's miserable out there," they engaged us in conversation. "You just came in by boat?"

"Looking for a pub, a place to eat and get out of the rain. Anything open this evening?"

"Come in for a bit." The man opened the screen door. "I am Dick. My wife Dorothy. Sit down, sit down. Get a load off." They pulled up some chairs. "So, where are you from?"

"We came in from Charlotte Amalie," said Dennis. "On our way to Florida. You live here?"

"We also came in on a boat, a little more than a year ago. We sailed for nineteen years and decided to stay here," said Dorothy. "We've been all around the world. Well, almost. Started out in San Francisco."

I became very interested in their story. "Did you sell your boat? About a year ago?"

"Yes, why?" asked Dick.

I don't know what prompted me to ask, "Was that a trimaran?" *Nineteen years...three quarters around the world... sold just over a year ago...* I had a premonition.

Dorothy leaned forward in her chair. "Yes a trimaran. Why do you ask?"

"Did you have a flag with Snoopy on a surfboard flying off the backstay?"

"You know our boat, the *SNOOPY*? Where? How?" They looked at each other, puzzled. Dorothy asked her husband, "Kenneth Helprin was his name, wasn't it, Dick? A tall, kind elderly man. He bought our boat." She turned to me. "Do you know him?"

I was as surprised as they were. It was as if a shiver went down my spine. "Do I know him? Ken is a friend of mine. I sailed with him until..." I stopped in mid-sentence. How could I tell them what happened to their boat?"

Dick and Dorothy looked at each other, then back at me. Dennis and Lambertus seemed to have guessed what was unfolding. They had heard my story of the *HAPPY TIME V*; well most of it.

Fascinated, without interrupting me, they listened to my tale, the wreck of the *HAPPY TIME*, formerly *SNOOPY*. Dorothy served tea with a shot of rum, and our visit lasted for more than an hour.

Before we left them, I wrote down the address of Mister Golden, Ken's friend. They wanted to get in touch with Ken.

Dick told us where we would find a tavern. "Might be closed, though. It's Saturday, and in this weather... Down by the dock is a grocery store. They have pretty much everything you need. They'll be open in the morning."

We said good-bye to our hosts. Dorothy had tears in her eyes. "Now we know the sad end of our *SNOOPY*." They probably talked through the night about the chance visit of some strangers and the news about the demise of their beloved boat. They had built it with their own hands, and I, unwittingly, brought the journey of their lives to conclusion. They learned where they could find the final resting place of their dream boat, their home for nineteen years: it's thirty miles south of Saba, in the Anegada Passage, on the bottom of the sea.

It was still raining as we walked the short distance to the pub, which was open. Aside from a few youths playing darts and drinking beer, the place was deserted. All we could get was a bag of potato chips and bottled Budweiser. The cold and uninviting atmosphere did not keep us for long and we walked back through the rain to the boat. To avoid the street on which Dick and Dorothy lived, we chose a different way. They might have had more questions, but I had no more answers.

The little grocery store near the dock was open early on Sunday morning. A few people were hanging out at the entrance under the awning. The rain had stopped, but the air was damp and uncomfortably cool.

Lambertus and I entered the store where we found lots of crates and cardboard boxes with yucca, eggplants, plantains and bananas. There were also mangoes, papayas and pineapple. On the half empty shelves were some cans of tuna fish and a variety of soups and stews, bags of rice piled up in a corner.

In front, under the awning, stood buckets filled with gladiolas and roses. Mother's Day—again a reminder of the *HAPPY TIME* disaster. The year before, on this day, Ken Helprin, Jeff Darren and I walked through the streets of Cumaná, watching children and grown-ups carrying flowers and gifts.

We picked items from the shelves and returned to the boat with tuna, corned beef,
noodles, stew and a bag of rolls.

Dennis found fault with our purchases. "Why the noodles? They need cooking, and there isn't much propane left. And the rolls look days old."

190

"You should have told us we don't have much propane," I said, "and the rolls are fine."

Lambertus nudged me. "Let's go back there and get some beer. Come with me?"

"One case is enough," Dennis called after us.

"Cheapskate," Lambertus mumbled on the way to the store. "We get two cases. Budweiser. He won't pay if we show up with Heineken."

We divided the expenses by three and Dennis grudgingly paid his share.

It began to rain again as we untied our lines from the dock. Dennis started the engine and turned the bow toward open water. A cold wind blew from the southwest. Barely out of the harbor, we hoisted the mainsail, set the jib and headed west.

I suggested we sail via the narrow passage between Culebra and Cayo de Luis Peña and pointed it out to Dennis on the chart. "We avoid all those rocks of Cayo Lobo and Lobito." I was surprised he even listened. "Otherwise we would have to take the Hermanos Passage, a big detour."

"Here, you take the helm. You run us aground, it's your funeral."

I had not expected that he would entrust the boat to me. On a beam reach, in fifteen to twenty knots of cold wind, the *CHANDELLE* picked up speed. Once past the shallows on starboard and the rocks on port, I put us on a northwesterly course. Alcarraza and Cayo Botijuela behind us, we left the Caribbean and headed for the Bahamas.

The rain ended in the afternoon and the wind died. Becalmed, on the mildly undulating sea, we motored toward Turks and Caicos.

During the night, Puerto Rico sank below the horizon. After midnight we experienced a thunderstorm with strong gusts. On watch from one to four a m, I had to

191

call Dennis to take down the Genoa and the mizzen. The wind increased to forty knots in rainsqualls. Before daylight, we met a southbound cruise ship, perhaps heading for San Juan. We saw how the big vessel pounded into the eight to ten foot seas. This weather continued into the afternoon, when again we were becalmed, and then the sky cleared.

"Feels good," said Lambertus. "Enough already with the bad weather."

"Depends what you call bad weather." Dennis could not engage in any kind of normal conversation.

*Obviously, wind is better than calm, but did it have to come at forty knots in a cold rainstorm?*

On May 14, under a sunny sky and in a pleasant light breeze, we passed Turks and Caicos too far off to see the islands. A big Korean fishing vessel was slowly steaming south. We came close enough to wave to the crew on deck.

Later that day, disaster befell the sailing vessel *PRIDE OF BALTIMORE*. We heard chatter on the VHF radio with regard to some emergency. Dennis switched to channel six, the marine safety channel, and we learned that the ship had capsized two hundred forty miles north of Puerto Rico.

The *PRIDE OF BALTIMORE* had left the Chesapeake in March of the previous year for a tour of Europe. She was on her return trip to take part in the tall ship reunion in New York's harbor on the Fourth of July. A thunderstorm had spawned a freak squall that took down the proud vessel in a matter of minutes. Later reports remarked that no precautions had been in place when the powerful gust had hit the ship. Knocked down on her beam-ends, hatches not securely closed, she quickly took on water and was unable to right herself. Of the eleven crew, four, including the captain, lost their lives.

At the time we had only incomplete information, but the news lay heavily on our minds. The unfortunate accident occurred in the area we had traversed a few hours before. It was a grim reminder that the ocean can turn into a deadly, invincible adversary.

The next twenty-four hours the weather changed between sunny and rainy, calm and stormy. Dennis was ill tempered and disagreeable, he seemed nervous or uncertain. Sitting at the SatNav, he punched in waypoints, then changed them, drew courses on the chart and erased them. He scratched his beard in that peculiar way of his, both sides at the same time, from the chin up.

We ran out of propane. I was in the process of preparing a tuna-noodle dish when the flame died. The pasta had begun to soften, but even for the most avid *al dente* gourmet, the core was still too firm. Leaving it in the hot water a while longer helped to some degree but made the noodles stick together while they remained raw inside.

Dennis' reaction was predictable. "You wasted our propane. We could have had coffee in the morning. Now we have to throw the food overboard. Can't eat that."

I opened two cans of Bumblebee tuna and mixed the contents into the half-cooked pasta. "Hmm, so good. I like the way this came out," I joked. "Don't you, Lambertus?"

"It melts on the tongue." He opened a can of beer. "Great with Budweiser."

We chewed the noodles, smacking our lips. Dennis, without a sense of humor, ate defiantly.

He found our antics foolish and became more irate. "Instead of buying food that doesn't need cooking, you bought noodles. And now we're out of propane. The rolls are already moldy. May as well throw those overboard, too." Then, with authority, "By the way, we're staying outside the Bahamas until we reach San Salvador Island. New course 345 degrees. Lambertus, you're up."

Turks and Caicos behind us, we approached Mayaguana. The weather became more settled and we enjoyed a steady breeze of fifteen knots from the southeast. I looked at our position on the SatNav and found that we were closer to the southern Bahamas than I thought. If Dennis wanted to stay east of the islands, we should change our course to 360, or due north.

In the afternoon of May 15 we passed Mayaguana at a distance of fifteen miles without seeing the island. We were heading directly for Samana Cay under full sail, making a comfortable speed of six knots.

Again Dennis changed his mind. He came into the cockpit and announced to Lambertus who was at the helm, "We leave Samana to starboard and head for the passage between San Salvador and Rum Cay. Course three oh five." He went back down into the cabin, mumbling something like, "damn SatNav. Can't trust that thing."

"What's the matter with him? Did you get that?" Lambertus looked at me, worried. "You better check that."

"I'll take a look at the chart and see what the SatNav tells me. Keep the course for now."

I went below and casually I looked over Dennis' shoulder. There were so many lines and crosses on the chart, I couldn't tell what's what. "What's our position, Dennis? Can I take a look?"

He seemed confused, scratched his beard in that funny way. "Why don't you stay out there and do as I tell you? Three oh five takes us just west of Samana Cay." He was downright nasty.

"You know, you really shouldn't talk to me that way," I told him and went back out to the cockpit.

Lambertus asked me, "Why does he think there's something wrong with the SatNav?"

"Oh, you heard him? The way he talked to me? I don't think he knows where we are. I tell you what: we give Samana a wider berth. Let's go on three zero zero.

That way we're not even coming close to the reef surrounding the Cay."

I went below for a nap and awoke around midnight. Dennis was at the helm. Sticking my head out the companionway, I immediately noticed a difference. Either the wind had changed, or we had changed course again.

"Take the wheel, Peter. I have to check the SatNav," said Dennis.

I took his place. *What the hell... Has he gone completely mad? Back and forth, port to starboard. Now this, now that...* The compass showed 340.

I no longer had any confidence in him. The man had sailed across the Atlantic from England, but that is different. There are no obstacles on the open ocean. No navigational skill is required, only guts, until you reach the islands.

He came to the hatch. "We are taking Samana to windward, leaving it to port. Keep her on three forty."

My eyes were still adjusting to the dark when I saw over the starboard bow a black line. *That's not the horizon.* I blinked, trained my eyes...

"Dennis, Dennis! Come up here, quick! Come up QUICK!"

From the companionway hatch he saw what I saw. "Diesel on! Diesel on!" He yelled. Lambertus was barely awake but ready to turn the key and press the starter button. The engine turned over and came to life. Dennis was at the helm in an instant, turning the wheel sharp to port.

At full throttle, the heavy boat came around sluggishly. Too late. The six-foot keel hit the rocks, hammering away, again and again, crunching and scratching on the hard coral and rock. An awful sound.

Dennis threw the Diesel in reverse, gave it full power. The keel was firmly jammed, trapped on the rocky bottom. Heeled over to starboard, in an unnatural angle, still pounding with every wave that hit the hull, the boat came to an abrupt halt.

Dennis continued running the Diesel, now in forward, then in reverse, to no avail. He shut the engine down and went below. It was just past midnight, Friday, May 16, 1986.

Reality overcame incredulity, wishful thinking and hope. Dennis gave in to momentary desperation. He was at a loss of what to do.

Lambertus and I had no immediate plan of action either. The tide was ebbing, the boat heeled more sharply to starboard, against the wind. Had we struck bottom at low tide, the rising flood might float us free, but that was not the case.

My first reaction was to check for leaks. A look into the bilge confirmed that we were not taking on water.

Dennis came quickly out of his lethargy and responded to the situation in a manner typical for him.

"Instead of calling me, you should have turned the boat around the moment you saw the reef. We lost precious time."

He did not directly accuse me; there was too much doubt in his tone. Still… *What is he trying to tell me? That it is my fault?*

"Had I done what you seem to suggest, and we hit the rocks anyway, then you could blame me."

"Damn SatNav, incompetent crew…" he mumbled. "Can't rely on anything."

"Anyway, it was still your watch."

"Get the sails down, first of all. What do we do then?" He still had not completely grasped the predicament we were in, or he was in a state of denial.

The tide continued to run out and the boat heeled in an unnatural angle into the wind. This made it very difficult to get the sails down. Lambertus stood at the mast and released the jib halyard while I gathered in the Genoa. Then, balanced on the slanted cabin roof, we succeeded in lowering the mainsail. Dennis stood in the cockpit as if paralyzed.

"He could at least take down the mizzen," Lambertus said under his breath, "or is he in shock?"

Lambertus and I worked well together, although he had no previous experience with boats. The mizzen presented no great problem to us.

"You should have spotted the reef sooner," Dennis grumbled.

"I came out an hour early. It was still your watch and you gave me the course to steer." I wanted to make that clear to him. "Anyway, why do you think there's something wrong with the SatNav?" I didn't think there was anything wrong with it.

"Gave me trouble before, that's all."

"Well, don't you think it's time to call the Coast Guard, or something?"

"Why? What can they do?" He scratched his beard. "We wait for high tide. That will get us afloat."

"It seems to me, we struck at high tide. So…" *Boy, is he dreaming?*

The sky became brighter in the east. We could make out the shoreline of Samana Cay. In some places rocks were visible—black, rugged rocks, waves breaking over them in white foam.

Half a mile from us, on the point of the cay, we saw the rusted, gutted hull of a small freighter, pinned to the reef. A couple of miles to the other side, the white hull of a sailboat lay high and dry on the beach, illuminated by the rising sun. Looks like a graveyard, I thought.

Dennis was below rummaging feverishly through his papers and ship's documents. He extracted a folder marked *Insurance*, and picked up the VHF. "PAN PAN." His voice shook as he spoke into the mike.

*PAN PAN* is the code word used in case of emergence without immediate danger to life or property. There was no answer.

"Great," he said and looked at me, accusingly. "You're always so smart, what would you do?"

"Try it again. Two consecutive calls are allowed."

When the second attempt was not answered, he called "MAYDAY."

*MAYDAY* is the emergency call used when life and property are in danger. BASRA, the Bahama Search and Rescue Association, responded promptly and Dennis reported the nature of our distress, location and number of persons on board.

BASRA turned the call over to the US Coast Guard. When there is no danger to life and limb, the Coast Guard does not get involved. Consequently, the matter was referred to a commercial salvage company, located on Sampson Cay in the Exuma chain. "A salvage crew will arrive in less than six hours," the Coast Guard informed.

Dennis placed a call through the marine operator to his insurance broker in Boston. In the lengthy conversation that ensued, he became increasingly agitated.

From the conversation, transmitted over the airwaves via the VHF radio, Lambertus and I learned that his insurance coverage had expired last April 30.

"Sorry about that, Dennis," said Lambertus.

I stayed away from him. There was nothing I could say to make the situation better, and I did not want to aggravate him. Obviously he did not want to talk to us.

"Let's stay out of his way," I said to Lambertus. "See how things work out. He needs some time by himself." We sat on the high side of the steeply inclined deck. There was hardly any wind and the sun was beating

down on us. "Want to swim ashore? It's only like what...
two hundred yards?"

"Sure." Lambertus was a good sport. We slid over
the side into the water. "Hey, I can stand. It's only six feet
deep."

I had to swim half the distance before I could touch
bottom, and then we walked in the fine white sand of the
beach the short distance to the wrecked freighter.

"Must have been thrown violently against those
rocks in a storm," I said as we contemplated the wide gash
torn into the port side of the ship.

"Yeah, and we managed that in a light breeze and
beautiful weather," Lambertus answered sarcastically.

Bleached driftwood, exposed by the low tide, lay at
the water's edge. Crabs scurried out to sea and starfish
dried in the sun. We walked back in the other direction to
see the stranded sailboat, but could not reach it. At one
point, the wooded interior of the island came down all the
way into the water and blocked the way.

"You hear that?" I stopped to listen. "A plane."

"There it is." Lambertus pointed out over the sea.
We did not expect rescue from the air, but there it was: a jet
at low altitude, the diagonal red stripe of the Coast Guard
on its nose. Just like the one that circled the *HAPPY TIME*
in the Anegada Passage. The plane made a wide turn and
disappeared toward the west.

"Dennis must have talked to them on the VHF," I
said. "They probably just verified where we were and that
we were safe."

We swam back to the boat and found Dennis
stretched out on the settee in the saloon. There was nothing
to do; there was nothing he could do but wait. On his face
was the expression of disappointment and resignation; of
failure, shame and disgrace over his  shortcomings. The
discovery that his insurance policy had elapsed was just
one more blow to his ego.

He sat up when we slid down the slanted companionway. "Where were you? We have an emergency here, and you leave the boat? Having fun, swimming around, walking on the beach? You are crew!" He vented his frustration on us.

"We checked out the depth of the water between here and the beach," said Lambertus, justifying our excursion. "There's six feet of water in the lagoon."

"And that's at low tide," I added. "Once the boat's off the reef, she might have enough water to float free."

"In the lagoon? You idiot! How do we get her out over the reef? Tell me that."

"There are always breaks in the reefs. Salvage people will know what to do. I don't think the situation is so hopeless." I took a can of tuna fish from the cupboard and turned to Lambertus. "You know where the can opener is?"

"What? You can eat at a time like this?" Dennis really got angry.

"I am hungry. And yes, I can eat when I am hungry. By the way, you just called me an idiot. Don't do that."

I opened the can, picked up a fork and went into the cockpit. Lambertus followed me. We sat on the combing on the high side.

Shortly after noon, a tiny plane appeared in the sky and came directly toward us.

"Look, a seaplane." We saw it before we heard it, the engine already throttled back for landing. It circled once and then set down on the calm water of the lagoon. Close to the *CHANDELLE,* the tall, lanky pilot stepped onto the sponson and dropped an anchor. Then he threw a line over to us. Lambertus caught it and fastened it to a cleat on deck.

Marcus Mitchell, a young man from Boston, had settled with his family on Sampson Cay in the Exumas, where he

200

established the only salvage company in the central Bahamas.

He stepped on board the *CHANDELLE*. "Marcus," he introduced himself and shook hands with Dennis. His companion was busy with ropes, pulleys and hooks. "That's Wayne. He will help us get you off this reef. Is there any damage to the boat? Any leaks?"

"Not so far," answered Dennis. "I don't know how deep some of the gashes may be."

Lambertus and I stood aside and listened.

"I tell you what we will do," said Marcus. "We can only work during a couple of hours around high tide. Secure everything inside as best you can. We may have to tilt the boat flat on her beam-ends and drag her into the lagoon. First I have to check how badly she is caught between the rocks." He combed his straight blond hair back with his hand. "They don't allow us to break more coral than what's unavoidable. You know, the environmentalists."

Wayne, a soft-spoken older man, politely asked permission to come on board. He knotted a long line to the main halyard and then jumped back onto the sponson of the seaplane. He rigged a sort of purchase, or come-along, a system of pulleys and rope. To the end of the line, he shackled a grabbling hook—a type of anchor with four prongs, often used to retrieve objects by dragging it over the bottom.

The tide was high at about two thirty in the afternoon. Wayne slipped into a wetsuit and, taking the hook with him, got into the water. He had to swim a hundred yards before his feet touched bottom. The halyard, from the top of the mast, with the added line and the purchase, almost reached as far as to the beach. He jammed the hook between some rocks and then took up the slack by working a lever attached to the come-along.

Marcus and Dennis discussed the procedure and other aspects of the operation. The cost must have been a main concern for Dennis, especially since he had no insurance coverage.

"We will try to get her off the reef," Marcus told him. "Then, on the sandy bottom of the lagoon, she'll be safer than on these ugly rocks."

Marcus inspired me with confidence. He went back to the plane and removed a wooden plank from the cargo space behind the cabin. Together with Wayne, who had come back from the beach, he wedged the two-by-four, covered with fire hose for cushioning, between rock and hull.

Lambertus and I helped Dennis put everything that could fall, break or damage on the starboard side, strapping in pots and pans as well as instruments, and locking or taping cupboard doors and drawers.

Marcus cautioned us to stand clear. "The halyard or the line could part. That could kill you."

Wayne swam back to the come-along. He started working the lever, a long handle that stuck out between the rocks in the waist deep water.

The line tightened, then stretched and groaned as it reached the breaking point. The boat, now inclined almost on her beam-ends, began to move.

Marcus raised his arm. "Stop!" he called out to Wayne, and to us, "We better get off the boat. I'll help Wayne. Go to the beach or whatever, stay away from the line. If it snaps… You know." He pushed his hair from his forehead. "If all goes well, if the line doesn't break, she'll slide right out of the gap where she's lodged her keel. She'll be in deeper water in no time. Until the tide turns. Then she'll sit on the bottom, but it's going to be a lot softer."

Reluctantly, Dennis followed Marcus over the side. Lambertus and I also got into the water. We swam to the beach where Marcus joined forces with Wayne on the come-along. The three of us sat on the warm sand, observing, hoping, wishing that this most critical part of the job went well.

"This guy seems to know what he is doing," said Lambertus. I nodded and had the same thought.

"If the port shroud breaks, she'll lose the mast. Then he is in big trouble." Dennis couldn't help making a negative remark.

Slowly, carefully, letting the small wavelets help by gently rocking the boat, Wayne and Marcus worked the come-along. They both put their body weight against the lever and, inch by inch, reeled in the line that seemed to be at its limit. Frequently they stopped to recover their strength.

There, what happened? The line had become slack; Wayne moved the lever effortlessly to reel it in.

Marcus wasted no time and swam out to the boat. He dove to check out the depth under her keel as she began rightening herself. Back on the beach, he shook hands with Wayne and smiled as he held out his hand to Dennis who ignored his gesture.

"How do you propose to get her back over the reef," Dennis snarled at him. "How do we get her into the deep water outside the reef, huh? Tell me that!"

"Whoa, whoa! Easy, man. Take it easy. I know this reef like the back of my hand. It will take up to a week, but we will get you out of here." Marcus kept his cool. "About a mile and a half from here there is a cut in the reef deep and wide enough at high tide to get you through. See where that white hull lies over there on the beach? Just before that. By the way, that's only half a hull. The other side is completely gone. You are lucky to have such a strong boat. Cutty Hunk, right?"

"Why should that take a week?" Dennis' tone was aggressive, impertinent.

Marcus remained calm. "There are sandbanks, shallows, rocks. Takes time. Maybe five days. We'll see how it goes."

We swam back to the boat where Wayne rigged a ladder so that we could get on board. Dennis sat with Marcus in the cockpit.

"How much is all this going to cost me?" Dennis asked.

I nudged Lambertus. "Let's go sit on the foredeck. We will hear soon enough how much this is going to cost him. Want to take a guess?"

"I have no idea. Five, six, eight thousand?"

"More than that, I imagine. I really don't know. He has no insurance; maybe Marcus will cut him a deal, but I doubt it."

Marcus and Wayne flew back home. They had to bring more equipment and the work was to begin the following day with the afternoon high tide.

We set a bow and stern anchor. As evening came, the boat began to heel and soon was again at a forty-five degree angle. The keel sat on the sandy bottom and there was none of that awful crunching, scraping noise, only the light swaying from the small wavelets that came over the reef into the lagoon.

The weather was mild and we slept soundly through the night. Only two days before, we sailed through a gusty rainstorm. The unfortunate *PRIDE OF BALTIMORE* capsized and sank in a capricious squall. While stranded at Samana Cay, we did not yet know of her ultimate demise, nor the fate of the crew.

In the morning, Lambertus said to me, he did not have the additional time it would take to bring the boat to Florida. "Seven days to get the boat out of here, and then two or three more to sail to Fort Lauderdale…"

204

"If you don't have the time, don't go sailing," I mocked him. "I always told my children, when they wanted to be back at a certain time, 'let's not go at all'. For sailing you need time, it's unpredictable. A lot of things can happen."

"I took three weeks off. That should have been enough to sail a boat from Antigua to Florida."

"Yeah, but as I said: a lot can happen—you see what I mean?"

"Yes, I see, but..." Lambertus shook his head. "Nevertheless, I'll ask Marcus if I can fly out with him."

"You gonna leave me alone with Dennis, the asshole? Hey, then I'll fly out of here, too."

Really, I did not like the idea of leaving Dennis in his predicament, but he was not a nice guy, someone I would want to be around. No friendship, no companionship and no food, no drink, no propane...

He was not abandoned. Marcus and Wayne were there and they asked if he needed anything. He would be okay.

By noon Marcus and Wayne returned to Samana Cay, setting the plane down smoothly in the lagoon. Besides fiberglass cloth and underwater repair compound, they brought bread, prepared meals and canned juices, soft drinks and beer. Wayne removed a rubber dingy from the plane and inflated it. Then he got anchors and line ready to begin work at the next high tide.

Lambertus approached Marcus. "I have to get back to Montreal. You think, I could fly out of here with you? No, not to Montreal! But maybe to Miami?"

"I fly you to Nassau for five hundred dollars. I can't fly to Miami, have no landing rights there."

I was standing near them. "Listen, Marcus, I don't want to stay alone with Dennis. You take us both for five hundred?"

"It's five hundred each. Not together, each." He turned away to show there was no negotiation.

I caught him by his arm. "What? That's a thousand dollars. No discount for two?"

"It's the going rate. A two and a half hour flight, and then I have to come back."

*Can I spend that much for a flight from here to Nassau? I've never been in a seaplane... Another week with Dennis on the stranded* CHANDELLE?

Marcus joined Wayne to help him with preparations for the job ahead.

"The going rate... as if there were scheduled flights from Samana Cay. Did you hear that?" I said to Lambertus.

"It's not cheap, but I have no choice." He went into the cabin to tell Dennis of his decision.

"All right, go ahead. You're no help here anyway," I heard him answer. All morning he has been lying on the couch.

Considering his character, it surprised me to see him so crushed. I would have thought him to be robust enough to deal with the situation more serenely. He was not the soft, emotional type, like Ken Helprin who had good reason to mourn the loss of his *HAPPY TIME*. But Dennis was clearly beaten.

I approached him. It was difficult for me but I said, "Dennis, I have decided to fly out with Marcus and Lambertus."

"What? You too?" He raised himself, leaning on one elbow. For a moment he looked at me. Then he slumped down again and did not say another word.

I sat in the cockpit with Lambertus. Dennis' disappointment touched me deeply. "I didn't think he would take it so hard. I feel very bad about it. But, hell, he has been such an idiot all the time. He didn't even try to make the trip pleasant. 'You are crew, you do as I tell you!'

206

Is that a way to treat us? What does he think we are? Slaves? Convicts?"

"You shouldn't feel bad. He had it coming." Lambertus had no deep emotional feelings; he lived on the surface of things. Nothing touched him. "He'll get over it. Maybe he will realize what a prick he is." He added, "Remember, he's the one who put us on this reef."

Well, that did not help me with my inner conflict. I went below, sat on the slanted companionway steps. "Dennis, you have Marcus and Wayne working with you. There really isn't anything I could help with. We would just get in each other's way."

"I have nothing to say to you. Pack your bags and get out of here. Don't bother me anymore."

"Okay, thanks. Your attitude makes it easier for me to leave." I went into the fo'c'sle, retrieved my duffel bag and put it next to Lambertus' pack and briefcase in the cockpit.

"When is Marcus leaving?"

Lambertus didn't know and shrugged his shoulders. "Now he's helping Wayne with something, but he has to fly back home this afternoon. Wayne will stay with Dennis throughout the procedure."

The *CHANDELLE* was afloat an hour before high tide at three o'clock. Wayne took over the operation. "We are in a deep spot here. We can drive the boat with the Diesel some fifty yards, then it's gonna get tough."

Dennis started the engine, put it in gear, but after only a few feet, the keel touched bottom. Wayne had taken an anchor far along the lagoon's deepest trough and winched in the line. Manpower and engine together moved the boat another twenty feet.

"Tide's still rising. We will gain at least a hundred feet before we hit a hump. Then we will have to wait until four in the morning."

"Come on, let's go. Put your bags behind the seats," said Marcus. Lambertus climbed into the back seat and I sat next to Marcus in the front.

"Put these on." Marcus handed us a pair of earphones. "It's pretty noisy." We accommodated ourselves in the small plane, which had room only for the pilot and two passengers. "And strap yourselves in."

Dennis had not come out of the cabin when we left the *CHANDELLE*. Our departure was very discomforting for me. I felt uneasy about leaving him and I needed to talk to lessen the burden upon my conscience.

"We came to sail, huh? Not to salvage a boat from a reef, right?" I tried to justify my action. "Lambertus, you don't have the time. You have good reason to leave, but don't you think that I should have stayed? I mean, didn't I have an obligation toward him? To help him in his dilemma?"

"What are you so sensitive about? The way he treated us, like forced labor... He's a despot, a tyrant. And a prick. Don't feel sorry for him. He got himself into that spot, it's his problem. Had he been, you know, not so hostile all the time, then it would have been different. So quit thinking about it."

*Not so easy for me. He has no scruples. But he is right, I should ease my conscience.*

Marcus revved the engine. Without so much as a bump, we slid over the calm water of the lagoon and hardly noticed as the plane lifted from the surface and became airborne. Looking down, we saw the *CHANDELLE* become smaller and fade into the distance. The outline of the reef and the beach slanted away. We gained altitude and Marcus curved toward Nassau.

"Rum Cay, Conception Island, Cat Island." Marcus spoke into the microphone and pointed to the various cays and islands. "Little San Salvador. Over there the Exumas will come into view in a minute. Sampson Cay, that's where I live. You can see Eleuthera on your right. I'll climb to three thousand feet."

There were few high clouds. In the crisp, clean air we could see the islands of the Bahamas spread out under us. The shades of the water ranged from dark blue to almost white near the beaches. The islands were clad in dark green foliage.

"The Tongue of the Ocean, almost ten thousand feet deep, that dark blue water far over to the left. And soon we are coming up on the Yellow Bank, just fifteen to twenty feet."

This world, this planet... Amazing! So much to wonder about.

"Directly below us is Highborne Cay, the northern Exumas."

Flying over the Yellow Bank, we saw the big, black boulders imbedded in light yellow sand. The shadow of the plane scurried over the ripples of the shallow water.

"We're almost there. Those are the Porgie Rocks at the eastern end of New Providence Island. I have to switch off now. I need the radio to listen to air traffic and get clearance for landing." Marcus curved over Nassau and descended parallel to the beach of Paradise Island.

To our right two huge, white cruise ships lay at the Prince George Wharf. Under us was Club Med and ahead was the Rainbow Bridge that connects Nassau with Paradise Island.

With hardly a splash, Marcus set the light plane down close to the beach on slightly choppy water and taxied to a ramp near the arrivals building of Chalks Airline that operated the big flying boats between Miami, Bimini and Nassau.

"I have to drop you off here," he said over the roar of the engine. "Go to the Immigration desk to get clearance. That's a thousand dollars for the two of you."

Lambertus handed him ten one hundred dollar bills. I had previously given Lambertus three hundred dollars and owed him two hundred.

"I'll send you the money as soon as I get to New York," I promised him.

We shook hands with Marcus who took off immediately. The tiny plane momentarily disappeared from view under the Rainbow Bridge and then lifted easily into the sky. Lambertus and I walked into the blue and white terminal building.

The Immigration official, a bossomy young woman in blue uniform, looked suspiciously at us over the counter. "Say again? You were what? Stranded where? So, where de boat? And who jus' brought you in here? Mhm, a plane. Whose plane? Overseas Salvage? Who they? Oh, de pilot lef'. Where he gone? Aha, took off, huh?"

"Let me try, Lambertus."

He had done his best to assure the woman that we weren't escaped criminals, smugglers or spies.

"Look, Madam," I said in a confidential tone, "the boat is still there, BASRA knows about it, the US Coast Guard knows it. There is nothing illegal here. We are not staying. We want to leave for Miami on the first available plane.

"You have passports?"

"Of course." We handed her our passports.

"You from Canada?" She looked at Lambertus, comparing his face to the photo. "And you from Germany? What you doin' here, baby?" Now she was amused and friendly. We laughed with her and filled out the immigration cards she gave us.

We had officially and legitimately arrived in the Bahamas.

There were seats available on the evening flight to Miami. Passengers were already boarding. We checked our bags on the tarmac where the bulky, yet graceful flying boat stood ready to roll into the water and turn into a powerful bird.

Lambertus and I chose window seats on the right side, he a row behind me. Many seats were vacant.

The two big Rolls Royce turbo-prop engines roared and the plane shuddered, restrained until the pilot released the brakes. Then, throttling back, the massive hulk turned toward the water's edge and slid into the element it would soon leave for another.

The aircraft rocked softly, finding its equilibrium, and we heard the wheels folding into the fuselage. Then full power pressed us back in our seats as the plane picked up speed and raced toward the Rainbow Bridge.

Under the bridge, still touching the water, it lifted the nose and quickly climbed skyward. Banking elegantly to the left over Paradise Island, we headed out over the ocean.

Andros Island, the biggest of the Bahamas, showed under the port wing. To starboard, in the distance, there were the South Berry Islands with Chub Cay, Whale Cay, Frazer's Hog and Bird Cay —places I had yet to visit.

Half an hour into the flight, we crossed over Bimini. Then only the Florida Straight separated us from our destination.

We touched down in the Port of Miami as the sun set in a beautiful glow behind the tall buildings of downtown.

"Here we are, Saturday night in Miami. What's your plan? I don't want to spend a night in a hotel in Miami."

"Let's go to the airport, first of all," Lambertus said resolutely. "See what our options are." Back on terra firma, he was again the secure, experienced business traveler.

A taxi, waiting in front of the Customs office at the port, took us to Miami International Airport. I booked a flight to La Guardia with a scheduled departure at eleven p m. Lambertus preferred a midnight flight to JFK, with connection to Montreal in the early morning.

I had an hour and a half before boarding. That gave us time for dinner in one of the airport restaurants. We chose one with tablecloths and napkins. Among the business travelers and weekenders, we stood out as a couple of beach bums in shorts and T-shirts. Lambertus looked even more ridiculous in his outfit and the briefcase.

*Whom should I call, The Cat or Julia? The Cat had actually been happy when I called from Antigua—or so she said. I'd better call Julia. So close to La Gardia, and that's where my car is.*

It was not too late yet to call. At a payphone, I dialed her number. "Hi, it's me. I'm in Miami."

"Oh? That was fast. I didn't expect to hear from you so soon."

"Yeah, well… I tell you about that when I get there. Listen, can I get in? My flight arrives around two in the morning. Leave the basement key, you know where?"

"En el florero, tu sabes. Okay?"

"Yes, I know. The planter outside. Thanks, and I'm sorry I called so late. See you in the morning."

"Buen viaje."

I hung up and joined Lambertus at the table.

"Everything okay?" he asked. "You know what it costs Dennis to get the boat out of the lagoon into deep water?"

"No. Did you ask him?"

"Marcus told me. They settled on ten thousand dollars. It was either that or two grand per day. Dennis must have figured it might take longer than five days, so he chose the flat rate."

"Wow, I bet Marcus gets it done in less than five days. However, they could run into some bad weather. Then, who knows? I don't think we'll ever find out."

"Marcus is a shrewd guy. He knows his business. He made a thousand bucks just flying us to Nassau."

"Five hundred dollars each... I think that's outrageous. That reminds me, do I have your address? I have to send you the money. Got a pen? Here, write it on the ticket envelope. I give you my address and number, too."

The time came to say good-bye.

"I'll give you a call when I am in New York. I have to go on business, sometimes," he called after me as I stood in line at the gate for my flight.

I slept late in the morning. Julia came downstairs once, but I did not move. The taxi from La Guardia had dropped me off at two thirty and I went to bed immediately.

It was almost noon when I went upstairs, freshly showered and clothed. Over lunch I told her of my latest adventure.

"So, I owe Lambertus two hundred dollars," I ended the story. "I think it's time for me to get my own boat. I really have to look into that, don't you think?"

I knew her opinion on that, but I had to hear her argument so that I could counter it.

"I should think you have learned what a risky life it is on the sea. You are lucky you're alive."

"I know, I know. What I have learned is what to do and what *not* to do. I won't go sailing in a half-rotten boat like that of Ken Helprin, or take chances with someone like Dennis. It's a matter of planning, having reliable equipment and using common sense."

"Even if you could buy your own boat, would you want to invest all you have in it?"

"All I know is that I am not ever sailing in other people's boats again." That was it—the deciding factor. If not in anybody else's boat, it had to be my own. *Because a boat it would be.*

"My life will be on the water, the ocean. It's my childhood dream. I can't ignore it. Sailing is my destiny."

"Oh my, oh my! I never knew you felt so strongly about it." Julia had no further argument to put forward, so she said, "Don't you need like a hundred thousand dollars for a boat like that? The one hundred thousand you don't have?"

"I will make it happen. You'll see."

# Epilogue

We knew it the moment we saw her. We felt it.

"Dad, she is perfect for you. And look, how well maintained."

This was the boat.

"Showroom condition," I said. "Twenty-seven feet, ten-foot beam. Standing headroom. I can't believe how roomy she is. The quarter berth; that's my bedroom. Diesel, modified full keel, wheel." Everything I wanted in a boat. "Propane stove. The head with a shower…"

"You will have to equip her for ocean cruising, though. But that you would have to do with any boat this size."

"Susi, I will buy this boat."

In August 1986, I wrote to my friend Jürgen in Germany:
*Remember die dicke Vineta? Remember*
*when we sailed out through the jetties into*

> *open waters and the Küstenwache sent us*
> *back? Remember sailing around*
> *Denmark? I am sure you do. Well, I am*
> *about to fulfill my life-long ambition. I just*
> *bought the boat in which I will sail as long*
> *as I am able to, or until I get sick and tired*
> *of the oceans.*

Jürgen was at the height of his career as a chemist at Bayer Pharmaceutical. Other priorities had taken precedence over his first love, sailing, but the longing was still there. He answered me, and I could read the nostalgia through the lines:

> *I am with you all the way. Write down your*
> *exploits. I want to read all about it. Good*
> *luck and congratulations! You are living the*
> *dream we once dreamed together.*

One day I came through Wilmington, Delaware, in my boat, which I had named *TRITON 3*. I called Aaron Orbin and Sylvia.

"I am in town, how about me coming up to say hello?"

The visit was cordial. Aaron seemed more at peace with himself. He had sold the *PRI HA GOFEN*. His new ambition was to breed a certain species of fish in ponds, then perfect the system and export the idea.

"I want to eradicate hunger in the world," he proclaimed. We had a seafood pizza—the best pizza I ever had.

It was sad for me to learn that Sylvia had cancer. A few months later I received the news that she had died.

Half a year after the reunion luncheon with Kenneth Helprin and Jeff Darren, Ken went on his world tour. He wrote me a letter from San Diego, where he had settled. "I traveled the world. Now I am writing a psychological self-help book, which I hope to publish."

When I called him to wish him luck with his book, he told me that he was about to get married.

I never heard from Jeff. I hope the mishap of the *HAPPY TIME* will remain the only one in his life.

In the years from 1986 onward, I have often stopped at Annapolis. Andrea Varta, who liked to call it 'Ann-uh-pew-lis, was a friend until she pressed me about information regarding her daughter Yvette and what went on during our voyage in the *VAMP*. I refused and told her, "Why don't you ask your daughter? It is not my place to interfere in your family matters." She never talked to me again.

All I know about Jeff Bourne is what Lynn Thordahl had told me. Whether he actually did get married, I never found out.

Lynn, however, practically integrated herself into my family, notwithstanding the fact that I was divorced. She even managed to get herself invited to my daughter's wedding, spent New Year's Eve with us—uninvited, I should add—and sailed the maiden voyage with me in my *TRITON 3*. Well, that was on my invitation and I was glad to have her on board. In the years that followed, we undertook several trips together.

No connection remained with Francisco Hobel or Ulf, owner and fellow shipmate of the *MACHETE*. I have little to say about Francisco. He is either the wimpiest or the most forgiving and tolerant character I have ever met. One thing I know: he is the richest person I ever had the opportunity to be associated with.

As for Ulf, I wonder how he is making his way through life.

I am sorry not to have pursued a friendship, nor remained in touch, with Nick Van Horn, owner of the *PETREL* and builder of the maxi-yacht we called the *105*. Once I asked his skipper, Frankie, if he would consider sailing to the Virgin Islands with me in *TRITON 3*.

"No," he laughed, "your boat is much too small for a voyage like that."

Well, then he would not be the right kind of guy for me, anyway.

Then there is Dennis O'Reilly. I believe he did not like to have friends. He did everything a man can do to avoid friendships.

I called him at his office in Boston a few weeks after I had left him at Samana Cay.

"Dennis, how are you? And how is the CHANDELLE? I am sorry about what happened and hope both you and the boat are all right."

"I don't have the time to talk to you," he said and hung up.

I guess, he is a very unhappy man—or is that his version of happiness?

And what about Lambertus de Boer? The first thing I did after my return to New York was to mail him a check for the two hundred dollars I owed him. Later we met twice in New York, when he was on business trips.

The Cat, no surprise, did not like the water. My predilection for boats, sailing and the ocean gradually separated us more. I seemed to have saltwater in my veins; she, on the other hand, was a city woman, a New York City woman.

I spent less time in New York as the years went by and eventually, what had become a once or twice yearly visit, dwindled down to once every other year. A life

218

dedicated to the sea precludes long-term relationships on land.

Through the years I owned and lived on *TRITON 3*, I enjoyed many happy sailing adventures with Julia, Susanne and Carlos.

My experiences, gathered in voyages from the *PRI HA GOFEN* to the *CHANDELLE*, prepared me for the years ahead; eleven years, to be exact.

*ELEVEN YEARS AFLOAT*
*My Life at Sea*